MUCH ENTERTAINMENT

In a letter to Dr. Samuel Johnson dated 29th May 1773, James Boswell urged his friend to make 1773 the year in which they carried out their much discussed project of visiting the Hebrides, 'which', wrote Boswell, 'I was confident would afford us *much entertainment*'.

MUCH ENTERTAINMENT

A Visual and Culinary Record of
Johnson and Boswell's Tour of Scotland in 1773

by Virginia Maclean

Liveright   New York

First published in the U.S.A. in 1973 by Liveright Publishing

ISBN: 0-87140-568-7
Library of Congress Catalog Card Number: 73-78865

Printed in Great Britain

Contents · Illustrations and Recipes

The owner or owners of the originals of the illustrations reproduced in this book are given at the end of this list of contents and can be identified by the small figure after each entry in the list.

	page
The Embrace, Rowlandson, 1786[2]	front endpaper
Walking up the High Street, Rowlandson, 1786[2]	front endpaper
Setting out from Edinburgh, Rowlandson, 1786 (frontispiece)[2]	ii
Tea, Rowlandson, 1786[2]	x
PLUM CAKE, and DUNDEE CAKE	1
Wit and Wisdom, Rowlandson, 1786[2]	2
ROAST GAME	3
Scottifying the Palate, Rowlandson, 1786[2]	4
CABBIE-CLAW, and CLAPSHOT	5
The Procession, Rowlandson, 1786[2]	6
SPICED APPLE PIE	7
Abbey of Arbroath, Paterson, 1813[3]	8
VEAL CUTLETS WITH WILD THYME, and PICKLED SALMON	9
Monboddo House, artist unknown, 1842[4]	10
COCK-A-LEEKIE, and MUTTON AND POTATO PIE	11
View of Castle Street in Aberdeen on a Market Day, Seaton, 1806[5]	12
SCOTCH BROTH, and POWSOWDIE	13
Slains Castle, Aberdeenshire, Daniell, 1822[6]	14
SALMI OF WILD DUCK	15
Nairn, Daniell, 1821[2]	16
HADDOCKS IN BROWN SAUCE, and CULLEN SKINK	17
Cawdor Castle, Beattie, 1838[6]	18
OATCAKES, and BAPS	19
View of Fort George and the Town of Inverness, Paul Sandby, 1744[6]	20
ROAST SADDLE OF MUTTON	21
Spinning with the Distaff, McIan, 1847[2]	22
CHOCOLATE BISCUITS, and CRISPY BISCUITS	23
A Highland Cottage (Dr. I. F. Grant's Collection), artist and date unknown[6]	24
CHICKEN STOVIES	25
Fort Augustus, Thomas Sandby, c. 1750[1]	26
FRICASSÉE OF PHEASANT, CHICKEN, OR RABBIT	27
Lodging at Macqueen's, Rowlandson, 1786[2]	28
LEMONADE, and GINGERBREAD	29
The Reconciliation, Rowlandson, 1786[2]	30
SILLABUBS, and OON	31
Revising for the Second Edition, Rowlandson, 1786[2]	32
POT HAGGIS, with NEEP PURRY	33
The Coolin, taken from Loch Slapin, Daniell, 1819[2]	34
FRIAR'S CHICKEN, and DROP SCONES	35
From the Isle of Raasay, looking westward, Daniell, 1819[2]	36
DIET LOAF	37
The Dance on Dun-Can, Rowlandson, 1786[2]	38
SCONES (VARIOUS)	39
Johnson and Boswell with Allan and Flora Macdonald at Kingsburgh, attrib. to Ramsay, no date[7]	40
GLASGOW PUNCH, and AULD MAN'S MILK	41
Gathering Dulse, McIan, 1848[2]	42
VENISON COLLOPS, and SKIRLIE	43
Dunvegan Castle, Griffith, 1772[6]	44
VENISON PASTY, and BRAISED HAUNCH OF VENISON	45
Angling, McIan, 1847[2]	46
POTTED HERRINGS, HERRINGS IN OATMEAL, and HERRING PIE	47
Grinding the Quern and Waulking the Cloth, Griffith, 1772[6]	48
BOILED GIGOT OF MUTTON, and CAPER SAUCE	49
The Recovery, Rowlandson, 1786[2]	50
BREAD AND BUTTER PUDDING, and VELVET CREAM	51
Carrying home the Peat, McIan, 1848[2]	52
CHERRY AND NUT TEABREAD, and SEED CAKE	53
Sailing among the Hebrides, Rowlandson, 1786[2]	54
TATTIES AN' HERRIN', and POTTED HOUGH	55
Johnson and Boswell with Rev. Hector Maclean, Kay, no date[2]	56
SHORTBREAD, and PITCAITHLY BANNOCK	57
The Island of Coll, with Fishermen and Boats, Poole, 1841[8]	58
QUICK WHEATEN BREAD, and ROAST LARKS	59
The White House of Grishipoll, Lauchlan Maclean, 1852[9]	60
ROAST GOOSE, and GROSSET SAUCE	61
Tobermory on the Isle of Mull, Daniell, 1818[2]	62
MINCED BEEF COLLOPS, and SOWANS	63

	page
View of Ben More from Ulva House, Daniell, 1817[2]	64
BRAMBLE, ROWAN, AND RIZER JELLIES, and MARMALADE	65
Remains of the Chapel on Inchkenneth, Daniell, 1817[2]	66
PARTAN PIE, and OYSTER LOAVES	67
Iona Cathedral, artist and date unknown (*c.* 1780)[6]	68
CLOUTIE DUMPLING, and CAUDLE SAUCE	69
Dr. Johnson in his Travelling Dress, Trotter, 1786[12]	70
JUGGED HARE	71
Lochbuie House and Moy Castle, G.E. (or E.G.), *c.* 1850[11]	72
Retouched tracing from the stone at Lochbuie House commemorating the 1773 visit. Drawn by Dr. James Maclean 1972[10]	72
HAIRST BREE	73
Girls Washing, McIan, 1848[2]	74
SALMON TROUT, and HOLLANDAISE SAUCE	75

	page
Inveraray Castle, Griffith, 1769[6]	76
VEAL FLORY, and ROUGH PUFF PASTRY	77
Loch Lomond, Hill, 1840[13]	78
SCOTCH TRIFLE, and RATAFIA BISCUITS	79
Glasgow Cathedral from Duke Street, Allan, 1835[13]	80
Punch Bowl from the Saracen's Head Inn, made *c.* 1770. An exhibit in the Old Glasgow Museum, photographed in 1972[14]	80
CREAM COOKIES	81
The Contest at Auchinleck, Rowlandson, 1786[2]	82
BURNT CREAM, and SCOTCH FLUMMERY	83
The Journalist, Rowlandson, 1786[2]	84
GAELIC COFFEE CAKE	85
Map of the Tour, by A. Carson Clark	86
A Breakfast Conversation, Rowlandson, 1786[2]	back endpaper
Chatting, Rowlandson, 1786[2]	back endpaper

The above illustrations are reproduced:
by Gracious Permission of
 1 Her Majesty Queen Elizabeth II
  and
by the Kind Permission of
 2 The Trustees of the National Library of Scotland
 3 Angus & Kincardine County Library
 4 Mrs. Ronald Lingen Hutton
 5 Aberdeen Public Library

 6 Edinburgh Public Libraries
 7 The Trustees of Dr. Johnson's House, London
 8 The Trustees of the National Gallery of Scotland
 9 Angus W. Maclean, Esq., and Harry Maclean, Esq.
 10 Dr. James N. M. Maclean of Glensanda, yr.
 11 Brigadier Alasdair G. L. Maclean of Pennycross
 12 The Trustees of the British Museum
 13 The Library of the University of Glasgow
 14 Old Glasgow Museum (The People's Palace)

Introduction

Two hundred years ago, Dr. Samuel Johnson, the great English lexicographer, and his young Scottish companion, James Boswell, made their famous tour of Scotland. Although both men published accounts of their journey, Boswell's *Tour to the Hebrides* is not only more detailed than Johnson's *Journey to the Western Islands* but it is regarded by experts in English literature as the finest travel book of the eighteenth century. Before the tour, Johnson had always affected to despise the people and the country of Scotland, but he returned, as Professor Frederick Pottle of Yale University has pointed out, 'with his prejudices much lessened, and with very grateful feelings of the hospitality with which he was treated'. Unlike Johnson, my fellow countryman, I never had any prejudices to overcome about Scotland. Indeed, I married a Scot, and I live in Edinburgh. Like Johnson, however, I have known the warmth and kindness of Scottish hospitality, and I enjoyed a great deal of it in the Spring of 1971 when, with my husband and three American friends, I made a tour of the places in the Highlands and Hebrides where Johnson and Boswell stayed. During that journey I had the idea of compiling this book. I had always taken a great interest in food, and on reading Johnson again I was stung by his assertion that 'women can spin very well, but they cannot make a good book of cookery'. It gave me that extra encouragement to write, if only to try to prove him wrong.

The purpose of this book is to illustrate Johnson and Boswell's tour, and to provide a selection of recipes for some of the meals they were given. Johnson was not always complimentary about Scottish food, but he frequently admitted that he enjoyed it; more often, perhaps, than is realized. Neither he nor Boswell ever recorded a recipe, but both gave details of what they had eaten. Their unaltered quotations on the subject of food formed the basis for my selection of recipes, the majority of which have been adapted for present-day use from traditional sources for Scottish cookery. These include: Mrs. McLintock's *Receipts for Cookery and Pastry-Work* (Glasgow, 1736); Mrs. Elizabeth Cleland's *A New and Easy Method of Cookery* (Edinburgh, 1759); Mrs. Hannah Robertson's *The Young Ladies' School of Arts* (Edinburgh, 1767);

Mrs. Susanna Maciver's *Cookery and Pastry as Taught and Practised at her Pastry School* (Edinburgh, 1773); Mrs. Frazer's *The Practice of Cookery, Pastry, Pickling, and Preserving* (Edinburgh, 1791); John Caird's *The Complete Confectioner and Family Cook* (Edinburgh, 1809); and Mrs. Margaret (Meg) Dods's *The Cook and Housewives' Manual* (Edinburgh, 1826); each referred to in the text by the author's name only.

The illustrations I have chosen represent cartoons, portraits, scenes and views connected with the tour. Finding views of buildings and places was not a simple matter, as many of them had been altered, or had fallen into ruin, or had been demolished since 1773. None the less, all the places illustrated in this book, even those which were drawn or painted long after Johnson and Boswell's deaths, are shown as they were at the time of the famous jaunt. Most of the views are by Thomas Sandby (1721–98), his brother Paul Sandby (1725–1809); David Allan (1744–96); William Daniell (1769–1837); Moses Griffith (*fl.* 1769–1809) who made the drawings for Thomas Pennant's *Tour in Scotland*; Robert Seaton (*fl.* 1780–1807); J. S. Paterson (*fl.* 1790–1821); William Beattie (1793–1875); David Octavius Hill (1802–70); and Paul Falconer Poole (1807–79). A few are by unidentified artists or, in one case, an artist known only by the initials G.E. (or E.G.). One drawing was done as an amateur sketch by a Prussian-Scot, Lauchlan Maclean (1805–79), when he visited Grishipoll in the Isle of Coll in 1852 to see the birthplace of his grandfather Archibald Maclean, who had emigrated to Danzig in 1753. The portrait of Flora Macdonald and her husband with Johnson and Boswell is attributed to Allan Ramsay (1713–84), and, in common with some other pictures in this book, has never been published before. Two other sketches of people are by John Kay (1742–1826) and Thomas Trotter (*c.* 1750–1803). The cartoons, all published in 1786, are engravings by Thomas Rowlandson (1756–1827) from drawings by Samuel Collings (*fl.* 1765–90). Lastly, the charming scenes of Highland life are by the historical illustrator Robert Ronald McIan (1803–56), and have been used where no other picture directly connected with the tour was available.

My general quotations on the tour have been taken mainly from Johnson and Boswell's own accounts, published in their lifetimes, but for extra information not given in those accounts I have quoted from the Yale edition of Boswell's *Tour to the Hebrides*. I have made no alterations, except to modernize spellings and punctuation, and to refer to Johnson as 'Dr.' on all occasions (although Boswell used 'Dr.' and 'Mr.' quite haphazardly). To avoid controversy, I have kept to the traditional term 'Scotch' for things, and have reserved 'Scots' for the people only.

Although the fullest understanding and appreciation of the tour can only come from reading Johnson and Boswell's accounts, my hope is that the illustrations and the recipes given in this book will encourage some of my readers to follow in their footsteps, and share the pleasure they discovered in the unchanging kindness of the Scottish people, and in the unspoiled and timeless Scottish scenery.

Detail from one of the damask napkins, 39″ long × 32″ wide, made in Edinburgh in 1748 for the wedding of Dr. Alexander Maclean of Rossal, Mull, and in use when Johnson and Boswell dined there on 21st October 1773 (see pages ix and 71).

Acknowledgments

I am indebted to many people for assistance in preparing this book. For providing or helping me to locate pictures my thanks are due to Miss Teresa Fitzherbert, of the Print Room in the Royal Library, Windsor Castle; Miss Elizabeth Ashley Cooper, of the Witt Library in the Courtauld Institute of Art, University of London; Mr. C. P. Finlayson, Keeper of Manuscripts of the Library of the University of Edinburgh; Mrs. Margaret Mellis, Senior Assistant, Special Collections Department of the Library of the University of Glasgow; Miss Ann Cameron of Inverness County Library; Miss Mary Smith of Angus and Kincardine County Library at Montrose; Miss E. Noble of Aberdeen Public Library; Miss C. L. Dickson (Scottish Room) and Mrs. N. Armstrong (Edinburgh Room) of the Central Branch of Edinburgh Public Libraries; and to the many officials, whose names I did not discover, in the National Library of Scotland, the National Gallery of Scotland; and the Department of Prints and Drawings in the British Museum.

For special help my thanks are also due to Professor Frederick A. Pottle, Ph.D., Litt.D., LL.D., Sterling Professor (Emeritus) of English, Yale University; Dr. Isabel F. Grant, M.B.E., LL.D., of Edinburgh; David Rutherford Boswell, Esq. (Boswell of Auchinleck); Mrs. Dorothy Margaret Booma, of Swampscott, Massachusetts; Brigadier Alasdair G. L. Maclean of Pennycross, C.B.E.; Herr Angus William Maclean (holder of the Iron Cross) of Berlin, and his brother Herr Harry Maclean of Heidelberg; Mrs. M. Clark, of Ullinish Lodge, Struan, Isle of Skye; Major Nicholas M. V. Bristol, K.O.S.B., of Breacacha Castle, Isle of Coll; Gordon P. Hoyle, Esq., Hon. Secretary of the Auchinleck Boswell Society; and Miss Margaret Eliot, Resident Custodian of Dr. Johnson's House, Gough Square, London.

I also express my appreciation to William Heinemann Ltd, and to the Editorial Committee for the Boswell Papers, Yale University, for their kind permission to quote from *Boswell's Journal of a Tour to the Hebrides with Samuel Johnson, LL.D., 1773*, edited by Professor Frederick A. Pottle and the late Dr. Charles H. Bennett, published in 1963.

Lastly, I am particularly grateful for the considerable help I have received from direct descendants of people who entertained Johnson and Boswell 200 years ago. These are His Grace the Duke of Argyll, T.D., D.L.; Dame Flora Macleod of Macleod, D.B.E., and her daughter Mrs. Robert Wolrige-Gordon of Hallhead; Mrs. Ronald Lingen Hutton (née Marjorie Burnett), who is descended from Lord Monboddo; Mr. Roland Clayton Booma, sr., of Swampscott, Massachusetts, who is descended from Captain John Macdonald of Breakish in Skye; and above all, my husband, Dr. James N. M. Maclean, who is the great-great-great-great-grandson of Dr. Alexander Maclean, of Rossal, Isle of Mull (later of Corrie-Kingairloch). My husband still owns two large damask napkins made for Dr. Alexander Maclean in 1748, which were in use at Rossal when Johnson and Boswell dined there is 1773. Without my husband's encouragement, and his help in the preparation and typing of the text, this book would never have been completed.

Edinburgh   Virginia Maclean

14th August   The Arrival of Dr. Samuel Johnson in Edinburgh

Dr. Johnson's Hosts: James Boswell and his wife Margaret Montgomerie

'Dr. Johnson,' wrote Boswell, 'had for many years given me hopes that we should go together, and visit the Hebrides. . . . In Spring 1773, he talked of coming to Scotland that year. . . . On Saturday the fourteenth of August, 1773, late in the evening, I received a note from him, that he was arrived at Boyd's Inn, at the head of the Canongate. I went to him directly. He embraced me cordially. . . . Dr. Johnson and I walked arm-in-arm up the High Street, to my house in James's Court: it was a dusky night: I could not prevent his being assailed by the evening effluvia of Edinburgh. . . . My wife had tea ready for him, which it is well known he delighted to drink at all hours. . . . He showed much complacency upon finding that the mistress of the house was so attentive to his singular habit.' Johnson was pleased with his young friend's home. 'Boswell,' he said, 'has very handsome and spacious rooms; level with the ground on one side of the house, and on the other four stories high.'

Rowlandson's cartoons, showing Johnson being greeted by Boswell and their walk up the High Street to Boswell's home, are given on the front endpapers.

Plum Cake

A traditional accompaniment to tea, adapted from Mrs. McLintock's recipe.

1 lb. (4 cups)[1] currants	½ level teaspoon nutmeg, and
8 oz. (2 cups) seedless raisins	½ level teaspoon ground
4 oz. (1 cup) chopped mixed	cloves
peel	*or* 1 level teaspoon mixed
2 oz. (½ cup) chopped almonds	spice
2–3 tablespoons brandy *or*	8 oz. (1 cup) butter
whisky	8 oz. (1 cup) caster (fine)
11 oz. (2¾ cups) plain flour	sugar
½ level teaspoon baking-powder	5 medium eggs
	¼ oz. caraway seeds, optional

Wash the currants and raisins; dry thoroughly on a cloth. Place in a bowl with the mixed peel and almonds, and leave to marinade (preferably overnight) in the brandy *or* whisky. Sieve the flour, baking-powder and spices together. Beat the butter until soft, add the sugar, and continue beating until the mixture is light and creamy. Very gradually beat in the lightly whisked eggs, adding a little of the sieved flour if the mixture shows signs of curdling. Fold in the prepared fruit and finally fold in the flour and caraway seeds (if used). Place in an 8-inch cake-tin, previously lined with greased paper. Bake in a pre-heated slow oven, Gas No. 2: 300°F., for 3–3½ hours, or until cooked. Remove, leave to cool for a few minutes in the tin, then turn out onto a wire rack. Remove the paper and leave until cold. Wrap, and store in an airtight container until required.

Dundee Cake

This can be made with the same recipe. Simply add 2 oz. (½ cup) chopped glacé cherries to the mixture, and arrange 1 oz. (¼ cup) split almonds in circles on top, *before* baking.

---

[1] Cup measurements for all recipes in this book are based on the 8 fluid oz. cup.

Tea, by Rowlandson
The Boswells watch with delight as Dr. Johnson takes more sugar for his favourite beverage. The yawn of the servant boy draws attention to the time: ten minutes after midnight.

15th–17th August   At James's Court, Edinburgh

Dr. Johnson's Hosts: James Boswell and his wife Margaret Montgomerie

At breakfast on 15th August Johnson met the Boswell's baby daughter Veronica. He spent that day and the following two days in the company of some of the most distinguished men and women in the capital, including the Duchess of Douglas, Lord Hailes, Dr. Adam Ferguson and Dr. William Robertson, the Principal of Edinburgh University. It was Robertson who, on 16th August, helped Boswell to show Johnson the main sights of the city. When they returned to James's Court they had a meal which had been specially prepared to please Johnson. 'We gave him', wrote Boswell, 'as good a dinner as we could. Our Scotch muir-fowl, or grouse, were then abundant, and quite in season, and, as far as wisdom and wit can be aided by administering agreeable sensations to the palate, my wife took care that our great guest should not be deficient.' Johnson, remarking generally on the tour, wrote: 'I passed some days in Edinburgh with men of learning, whose names want no advancement from my commemoration, or with women of elegance, which perhaps disclaims a pedant's praise.' Peter Pindar, in his *Poetical and Congratulatory Epistle*, a parody on the tour published in 1786, put the following words in Boswell's mouth:

> While Johnson was in Edinburgh, my wife
> To please his palate, studied for her life,
> With ev'ry rarity she fill'd her house,
> And gave the Doctor for his dinner, grouse.

Rowlandson's cartoons, showing Johnson at breakfast with Veronica Boswell, and late at night after a day chatting with learned men, are given on the back endpapers.

Roast Game

Grouse, partridge, and pheasant. The game seasons in Scotland are as follows:

Grouse, 12th August ('The Glorious Twelfth') to 10th December; partridge, 1st September to 1st February; and pheasant (and the rare capercailzie) 1st October to 1st February. Only young birds are suitable for roasting. Older game should be used for casseroles, stews, pâtés, and skinks (soups). The flavour and texture of game is improved if it is hung for three to ten days in a cool place, the time depending on the age of the bird, and on how 'gamey' a flavour is required.

2 grouse *or* 2 partridges, *or* 1 pheasant	*for the bread croûtes*
4 oz. ($\frac{1}{2}$ cup) butter	2 slices white bread
salt and pepper	2 oz. ($\frac{1}{4}$ cup) butter
4 large rashers fat bacon	game livers
$\frac{1}{2}$ pint ($1\frac{1}{4}$ cups) giblet stock	pinch of thyme
	$\frac{1}{2}$ small onion, finely chopped

Wipe the birds. Season inside and out with salt and pepper, and truss. Place a little butter in each bird, spread the rest on the breast, and cover with fat bacon. Make a giblet stock, keeping back the livers. Place the birds in a roasting-tin, and cook (basting occasionally) in a fairly hot oven, Gas No. 5: 375°F., 25–35 minutes for grouse (do not overcook); 30–35 minutes for partridge; 45–50 minutes for pheasant. Five minutes before the end of the roasting time, remove the bacon, sprinkle the breast with flour, baste well, and return to the oven to 'froth'. Remove, and keep warm. Drain the fat from roasting-tin, leaving juices. Add giblet stock, simmer, season well, and skim, if necessary. Pour into sauce-boat.

BREAD CROÛTES   Remove the crusts, fry the slices of bread in butter until golden, and keep warm. Finely chop the livers, and cook in the butter with the thyme and onion. Season, and spread on the bread croûtes. Place the croûtes on a hot ashet (dish). Place the birds on the croûtes. Garnish with watercress or green salad, and game chips. Serve with skirlie (see p. 43) and rowan jelly (see p. 65) or cranberry jelly. Serves 4.

18th August Edinburgh to St. Andrews, stopping *en route* at Leith, Inchkeith, Kinghorn and Cupar

Host: The landlord of Munro's Inn, Kinghorn, Fife

On 18th August 1773, the *Edinburgh Evening Courant* carried the following notice: 'Edinburgh. Last Saturday arrived here on a visit to James Boswell, Esq., the celebrated Samuel Johnson, Esq.; and this day they set out for Sir Alexander Macdonald's in the Isle of Skye.' That morning Johnson and Boswell, with Boswell's Bohemian servant, Joseph Ritter, bade farewell to Mrs. Boswell and began their famous tour. At Leith on the shore of the Firth of Forth they stopped to eat, and Boswell tempted Johnson to enjoy a new taste. 'I bought', wrote Boswell, 'some *speldings*, fish (generally whitings) salted . . . and dried in the sun, and eaten by the Scots by way of a relish. He [Johnson] had never seen them, though they are sold in London. I insisted on *scottifying* his palate; but he was very reluctant.' They then crossed the Forth by ferry, breaking their passage on the way over to Fife so that Johnson could land on the island called Inchkeith, where 'he stalked like a giant among the luxuriant thistles and nettles'. After landing at Kinghorn in Fife they dined 'at Munro's, on fish with onion sauce, roast mutton, and potatoes'. From Kinghorn to St. Andrews they took a post-chaise, stopping only once, at Cupar, to have tea. 'We had', wrote Boswell, 'a dreary drive, in a dusky night, to St. Andrews, where we arrived late.' Johnson, by contrast, appeared to enjoy the drive, and wrote: 'The roads are neither rough nor dirty; and it affords a southern stranger a new kind of pleasure to travel so commodiously without the interruption of toll-gates. . . . The carriages in common use are small carts, drawn each by one little horse.'

Rowlandson's cartoon, showing Johnson, Boswell and Ritter taking their leave of Mrs. Boswell, is given as the frontispiece.

Cabbie-Claw

This dish was praised by Captain Edward Topham, an English visitor to Edinburgh in 1774. Egg sauce, an essential part of Cabbie-Claw, would probably have more appeal to modern taste than the onion sauce given to Johnson and Boswell.

1 very fresh small codling, $2\frac{1}{2}$–3 lb.
1 tablespoon coarse salt
small bunch parsley
1 tablespoon grated horseradish
$1\frac{1}{2}$ lb. cooked potatoes, mashed with butter

for the garnish
chopped parsley, and paprika pepper

for the egg sauce
1 oz. butter
1 oz. flour
$\frac{1}{2}$ pint ($1\frac{1}{4}$ cups) fish bree (stock)
$\frac{1}{4}$ pint ($\frac{2}{3}$ cup) top of milk
2 hard-boiled eggs

Clean and skin the fish; remove the eyes. Dry, and rub all over with coarse salt. Leave to stand overnight. Hang up in the open air, ideally in a breeze away from the sun, for 24 hours. Place in a pan of boiling water with the small bunch of washed parsley and grated horseradish, and simmer slowly until cooked, about 25–30 minutes. Remove carefully with a fish-slice onto a board, divide into large flakes, taking care to remove the bones. Arrange the hot mashed potatoes in a circle on a hot ashet. Place the flaked fish in the centre, cover, and keep warm.

EGG SAUCE   Melt the butter in a small saucepan, stir in the flour, and cook for a minute without colouring. Gradually stir in the milk and fish bree, and stir to the boil. Simmer for 3–4 minutes. Chop the hard-boiled eggs, and mix into the sauce. Check the seasoning, and pour the sauce over the flaked fish. Sprinkle on a little chopped parsley and paprika pepper. Serves 4–6.

Clapshot
Mrs. Dods wrote: 'Turnip and potato mixed together eat well with boiled or roast mutton.' Johnson and Boswell had potatoes only with their roast mutton. Take equal quantities of turnips and potatoes, cook separately, and drain well. Mash each vegetable until smooth, mix together, add butter and seasoning, reheat, and serve very hot. Clapshot goes well with Pot Haggis (see p. 33).

Scottifying the Palate, by Rowlandson
Fishwives on the shore of the Forth watching Boswell trying to tempt Johnson with speldings

Host: Dr. Robert Watson, Professor of Logic, St. Andrews University

Arriving late in St. Andrews on the night of 18th August, the travellers (as Johnson and Boswell will often be called) went first to Glass's Inn, where, wrote Boswell, 'we found a good supper.— Rissered haddocks and mut. chops.' From the inn they walked through the dark streets to St. Leonard's College, the residence of Dr. Watson, with, said Boswell, 'the landlord walking before us with a candle, and the waiter with a lantern'. They found 'very comfortable and genteel accommodation' in the home of Dr. Watson, with whom they stayed while they were in St. Andrews. On 19th August, wrote Johnson, 'we rose to perambulate a city, which only history shows to have once flourished, and surveyed the ruins of ancient magnificence. . . . The professors who happened to be resident in the vacation made a public dinner, and treated us very kindly and respectfully,' the meal consisting of 'salmon, mackerel, herrings, ham, chicken, roast beef, apple pie.' During dinner, said Boswell, 'we talked of change of manners. Dr. Johnson observed that our drinking less than our ancestors was owing to the change from ale to wine. . . . I was much pleased to see Dr. Johnson actually in St. Andrews, of which we had talked so long.' They left the city at about noon on 20th August.

Spiced Apple Pie

Adapted from a recipe by Mrs. Frazer, who wrote: 'Pare, quarter and core the apples and season them with sugar, beat cinnamon and the grate of a lemon. If you wish to have your pie very rich, put in some ston'd raisins, blanch'd almonds, citron and orange peel, cut down; cover it with puff'd paste. Don't be sparing of sugar to any fruit pie.'

Sweet Pastry
8 oz. (2 cups) plain flour
pinch of salt
3 oz. ($\frac{3}{8}$ cup) butter *or* margarine
2 oz. ($\frac{1}{4}$ cup) lard *or* cooking fat
1 rounded dessertspoon caster
  (fine) sugar
1 tablespoon cold water
alternatively: Rough Puff Pastry
  (p. 77)

Filling
1$\frac{1}{2}$ lb. cooking apples
3 oz. (approx. $\frac{1}{2}$ cup) sugar
1 level teaspoon cinnamon
grated rind and juice of 1
  lemon
1 oz. ($\frac{1}{4}$ cup) split almonds
2 oz. ($\frac{1}{2}$ cup) mixed peel,
  shredded
2 oz. ($\frac{1}{2}$ cup) seeded raisins

SWEET PASTRY Sieve the flour and salt into a bowl. Add the fats, and rub in until the mixture resembles fine breadcrumbs. Dissolve the sugar in the cold water, and mix to form a stiff dough. Cover, and leave to rest in a cool place while the filling is prepared.
FILLING Peel, core, and thickly slice the apples into a bowl. Add the sugar, cinnamon, lemon rind and juice, almonds, shredded mixed peel, and raisins (which, to plump up, have been steeped in boiling water for a few minutes, and then drained). Mix all together, and place in a medium-sized pie-dish, and add about 2 tablespoons of cold water.
TO COMPLETE On a lightly-floured board roll out the pastry so that it is large enough to cover the dish. Damp the rim of the pie-dish. Lift the pastry on a rolling-pin, and lay it over the filling, press down, trim the edge, decorate the edge with a fork, and make a hole in the centre of the pastry. Sprinkle sugar on the top. Bake in a pre-heated hot oven, Gas No. 6: 400°F., for 30–40 minutes. Serve hot with cream. Serves 4–6.

The Procession, by Rowlandson
Guided by a waiter and the landlord of Glass's Inn, Johnson and Boswell make their way to St. Leonard's College

Abbey of Arbroath, by Paterson
Washer-women drying sheets near Arbroath Abbey, where Scotland's
independence was declared in 1320

20th August   St. Andrews to Montrose, stopping *en route* at Dundee and Arbroath

Host: William Driver, landlord of the Ship Inn, High Street, Montrose

After leaving St. Andrews, 'our way', wrote Johnson, 'was over the Firth of Tay, where, though the water was not wide, we paid four shillings for ferrying the chaise. ... We stopped a while at Dundee, where I remember nothing remarkable, and mounting our chaise again, came about the close of the day to Arbroath.... The monastery is of great renown in the history of Scotland. Its ruins afford ample testimony of its ancient magnificence.' The renown of the Abbey or monastery of Arbroath rests partly on its association with the Scottish Declaration of Independence, which was signed by the King and his Parliament in the Regality Chamber of the Abbey in 1320. Arbroath and its scenes were immortalized in *The Antiquary* by Sir Walter Scott. Johnson himself stated: 'I should scarcely have regretted my journey, had it afforded nothing more than the sight of Arbroath. ... Leaving these fragments of magnificence, we travelled on to Montrose.' In Montrose 'we found', wrote Boswell, 'but a sorry inn, where I myself saw [a] waiter put a lump of sugar with his fingers into Dr. Johnson's lemonade, for which he called him "Rascal!". It put me in great glee that our landlord was an Englishman.' At this place, the Ship Inn, where the travellers stayed the night, they 'dined on haddocks, pickled salmon, veal cutlets, and fowl'. Before they left Johnson was provoked by the well-meaning Boswell, who recalled that Johnson 'was angry at me for proposing to carry lemons with us to Skye, that he might be sure to have his lemonade.' 'Sir,' said Johnson, 'it is very bad manners to carry provisions to any man's house, as if he could not entertain you. To an inferior, it is oppressive; to a superior, it is insolent.'

Veal Cutlets with Wild Thyme

According to Mrs. Dods 'Dr. Johnson liked lemon with his veal.'

4 veal cutlets *or* escalopes	¼ pint (⅔ cup) sour cream
salt and pepper	few sprigs wild thyme, chopped
2 oz. (¼ cup) butter	juice of ½ lemon

Trim the cutlets, and sprinkle with salt and pepper. Melt the butter in a pan until fairly hot. Place the cutlets in the pan, seal the outsides, lower the heat, and continue cooking for 8–10 minutes in all. It escalopes are used, cook for 6–8 minutes. Remove onto a hot ashet. Add the sour cream to the juices in the pan, and simmer for 5 minutes. Add the thyme and lemon juice, reheat, and season with salt and pepper. Pour this sauce over the cutlets. Serve hot. Serves 4.

Pickled Salmon

'To pickle Salmond,' wrote Mrs. McLintock, 'take a fresh Salmond, cut it in Pieces, boil it neither too much nor too little, put a Handful of Salt in the Water, then take it out and let it cool; then take of the best white Wine Vinegar a Pint, a choppen of Water, half a Ounce of White Pepper, half an Ounce of Ginger, half an Ounce of Jamaica Pepper and a handful of Salt, boil all those together, till the Pickle taste well of the Spice, let it cool, and put the Salmond into the cask where you keep it, pour the Pickle on it when it is cold, and keep it for Use, put a little Oil of Cloves on it, and cover it very close.'

Sauce for Pickled Fish

Mrs. Frazer wrote: 'Take parsley and chives, of each an equal quantity, some anchovies and capers, shred very small, with a little salt, pepper, nutmeg, oil and vinegar, all mix'd well together; when you dish the fish, pour some of this sauce upon them, and serve the rest of it in a China basin.'

21st August Montrose to Aberdeen, stopping *en route* at Laurencekirk and Monboddo House

Host: James Burnett, Lord Monboddo

Before leaving Montrose on the morning of 21st August, Boswell sent his servant Joseph ahead to Lord Monboddo, the judge, to find out if it was convenient to call on him. 'As we travelled onwards from Montrose,' wrote Boswell, 'we had the Grampian Hills in our view, and some good land around us, but void of trees and hedges. . . . We stopped at Laurencekirk . . . Dr. Johnson observed they thatched well here. . . . About a mile from Monboddo, Joseph was waiting to tell us my lord expected us to dinner. We drove over a wild moor. Lord Monboddo received us at his gate most courteously. . . . His lordship was dressed in a rustic suit, and wore a little round hat; he told us we now saw him as *Farmer Burnett*, and we should have his family dinner, a farmer's dinner,' which consisted of 'admirable soup, ham, peas, lamb, and moor-

fowl'. Johnson remarked: 'I have done greater feats with my knife than this;' although, as Boswell noted, 'he had eaten a very hearty dinner'. Johnson was delighted with Lord Monboddo: 'The magnetism of his conversation easily drew us out of our way, and the entertainment which we received would have been a sufficient recompense for a much greater deviation [from the main route].' After leaving Monboddo House, the travellers had a tedious drive to Aberdeen, where they arrived at half-past eleven at night. Although they were told that the New Inn was full, they managed to get 'comfortless' accommodation there for the night. For supper, Boswell said they had 'a broiled chicken, some tarts, and crabs' claws'.

Cock-a-Leekie

'This soup,' wrote Mrs. Dods, 'must be very thick of leeks, and the first part of them must be boiled down into the soup until it becomes a lubricous compound.'

1 boiling fowl	faggot of herbs
2–3 bunches leeks, about 2 lb.	(bouquet garni)
5 pints of water	16 prunes, soaked
salt and pepper	chopped parsley

Prepare the fowl and wipe well before trussing. Wash, trim and clean the leeks thoroughly, discarding the coarse outside leaves. Chop into small pieces, about $\frac{1}{2}$ inch in size. Place the fowl and giblets into a large pan, cover with water, bring slowly to the boil, and skim well. Add $\frac{3}{4}$ of the prepared leeks, salt and pepper, and faggot of herbs. Stir well, cover, and leave to simmer for about

3 hours (depending on the age of the fowl). Lift out the fowl and giblets, allow the soup to cool a little, and remove any grease from the top. Add remaining leeks, and the soaked prunes (stones removed), and simmer for a further 30 minutes. Check the seasoning, and add some of the fowl, which has been diced. Sprinkle with parsley, and serve hot. Serves 6–8. For a more substantial meal, cut the fowl into small joints, and add to the soup. Reheat, and serve.

Mutton and Potato Pie

To make this farmer's dinner, Mrs. Cleland wrote: 'Take a Breast of Mutton and cut it into Steaks, season it with Pepper and Salt; Lay a Lair of Mutton and a Lair of Potatoes scraped and sliced, then a Lair of sliced Onion, so go on till you fill the Dish; season them between every Lair; cover it with Puff Paste; two Hours bake it; put a Piece of sweet Butter in it and Gravy, when it comes out of the Oven.'

Monboddo House in 1842, artist unknown
This was the building as Johnson and Boswell knew it. When it was reconstructed in 1866, the dining-room was left unchanged.

21st–24th August   At the New Inn, Aberdeen

Host (for dinner on 23rd August) : Sir Alexander Gordon, Bt., Professor of Medicine, King's College, Aberdeen

On their first morning in the city, Johnson and Boswell were joined for breakfast by Professor Thomas Gordon, who afterwards accompanied them to the English Chapel, where he took the service. Later that day another professor, Sir Alexander Gordon, was their guest for dinner at the New Inn. The meal consisted of 'skate, roasted lamb, roasted chickens, and tarts,' and 'Dr. Johnson ate several platefuls of Scotch broth, with barley and peas in it, and seemed very fond of the dish.' Boswell remarked: 'You never ate it before,' to which Johnson replied: 'No, sir; but I don't care how soon I eat it again.' Indeed, Johnson was so pleased with the dish that in a letter to one of his friends he had no hesitation in stating that 'barley broth is a constant dish, and is made well in every house'. The next day, 23rd August, the travellers spent part of the morning at Marischal College in new Aberdeen before making their way to the Town Hall, where, at one o'clock, the Lord Provost, James Jopp, conferred the Freedom of the City upon Johnson. In the afternoon, the new Freeman went with Sir Alexander Gordon to see King's College in old Aberdeen, while Boswell visited some personal friends with Thomas Gordon. That evening they were guests at a special dinner given in their honour by Sir Alexander Gordon at his home. Among those present were the Lord Provost and several leading academics, including the Principal of King's College, Professor Roderick Macleod, whose elder brother, Colonel John Macleod of Talisker, acted as their host when they reached Skye. They left the city early on the following day.

Scotch Broth

1 oz. dried peas, soaked	1 small turnip, diced
2 oz. barley	2 leeks, chopped
1 scrag end of mutton, $1\frac{1}{2}$ lb.	1 large onion, chopped
salt and pepper	2 sticks celery, diced
3 pints water	$\frac{1}{4}$ small cabbage, shredded
2 large carrots, diced	2 tablespoons chopped parsley

Soak the peas overnight. Place the peas, barley, and mutton in a pot, add the cold water and bring to the boil. Skim well, add the salt and pepper, and leave to simmer for one hour. Add the diced carrots, turnips, leeks, onion, and celery, and simmer for a further hour. Add the cabbage, and simmer for a further 15 minutes. Remove the scrag end, cut off the meat, and chop into small pieces. Return to the soup, reboil, skim off any grease, add plenty of chopped parsley, check the seasoning, and serve very hot. Serves 4–6. If the meat is to be served as a separate course, use $1\frac{1}{2}$–2 lb. of middle neck of mutton instead of scrag end; remove from the broth, and divide into cutlets before serving.

Powsowdie (or Sheep's Head Broth)

As above, using 2 extra pints of water, and one prepared and split sheep's head instead of the scrag end. Before cooking, remove the brains, soak them in cold salted water and simmer separately for 10 minutes; then drain and chop. When the soup is cooked, remove the head, slice the meat and tongue, and serve as a main course with parsley sauce. Add the meat trimmings and brains to the broth, and serve as for Scotch Broth.

MUTTON BROTH   Mrs. Cleland wrote: 'Take about six Pounds of Mutton, boil it in three Scots Pints [12 Pints] of Water, with sweet Herbs, Onions, two or three Turnips, a Quarter of a Pound of fine Barley or Rice, Salt and Pepper; a little before you take it up, put in a handful of chopped Parsley.'

View of Castle Street in Aberdeen on a Market Day, by Seaton
The New Inn, where Johnson and Boswell stayed, is on the left

13

Slains Castle, Aberdeenshire, by Daniell
'Built on the margin of the sea', but now a ruin

24th August   Aberdeen to Slains Castle, stopping *en route* at Ellon

Hosts: James Hay (formerly Boyd), 15th Earl of Erroll, Lord High Constable of Scotland, and his second wife, Isabella Carr, Countess of Erroll

The first stop the travellers made after leaving Aberdeen was at the New Inn at Ellon for breakfast. They then moved on to the home of Lord Erroll at Slains Castle. 'We had', wrote Boswell, 'received a polite invitation to Slains Castle. We arrived there just at three o'clock, as the bell for dinner was ringing. . . . Lady Erroll received us politely, and was very attentive to us during the time of dinner', after which she 'favoured us with a sight of her young family, whom she made stand up in a row.' Lord Erroll was not there when the travellers arrived, and did not come in until nine in the evening, but both were well looked after by his wife and his brother, Hon. Charles Boyd, who was on a visit from Aberdeen. For entertainment, Lady Erroll ordered a coach to take Johnson and Boswell for a drive; and they went first to Dunbuy, 'a rock near the shore quite covered by sea-fowls,' and then to the Bullers of Buchan or 'The Pot', a local maelstrom, upon which they sailed in a hired boat. On their return to the castle they found 'coffee and tea in the drawing-room'. Both travellers thought the castle was very elegant inside, and impressive outside, as it stood on the margin of the sea. No trees grew in the locality, but Lord Erroll had 'cultivated his fields so as to bear rich crops of every kind'. In the evening they had a long talk with Lord Erroll, with whom Johnson had once dined in London. Both had a comfortable night, although Boswell complained about the pillows, which 'were made of the feathers of some sea fowl' and had 'a disagreeable smell'.

Salmi of Wild Duck

No comment was made by either traveller on what they ate at Slains, but the mention of local sea-fowls suggested the recipe for this page. The season for wild duck is from 1st September to 28th February. Widgeon and teal are of the same family, but smaller. All require hanging for several days before cooking, and all can be roasted when young. They should be kept slightly underdone for the best flavour. Wild duck needs to be roasted in a hot oven for about 40 minutes; widgeon and teal for about 25–30 minutes. Serve with thin gravy, watercress, and orange salad. Although the recipe below is for wild duck, grouse, partridge and pheasant can be cooked in the same way.

2 ducks, cleaned and trussed	1 level tablespoon flour
salt and pepper	1 wine glass of red wine
2 oz. ($\frac{1}{4}$ cup) butter	juice of $\frac{1}{2}$ lemon
1 onion, sliced	1 orange, peeled and segmented
bay leaf and thyme	1 bunch watercress, washed

Season the ducks well. Cover the breasts with 1 oz. butter, and roast in a hot oven, Gas No. 6: 400°F., for 25 minutes until $\frac{3}{4}$ cooked. Remove, cool, and carve into slices. Cover the meat to prevent drying. Chop the bones and trimmings, and place with 1 pint of water in a pan. Add the onion, bay leaf, thyme, and the juices from the roasting-tin, and simmer for 1 hour to extract flavour. Strain, and reduce to about $\frac{1}{2}$ pint. In the meantime, melt 1 oz. butter, add the flour, and cook the roux slowly until brown. Gradually stir in the stock, bring to the boil, add the wine, and simmer for 10 minutes. Add the lemon juice, and check the seasoning. Add the orange segments (having removed all the pips), add the sliced duck, and reheat without boiling. Serve on a hot ashet, and garnish with watercress. Serves 4.

SAUCE FOR WILD FOWL   Mrs. Frazer wrote: 'Take a quantity of veal gravy according to the bigness of your dish of wild fowl, season it with pepper and salt; put in the juice of two oranges, and a little claret. This will serve all sorts of wild fowl.'

Nairn, by Daniell
Where Johnson and Boswell had breakfast on 27th August 1773

25th–27th August   Slains Castle to Nairn, stopping *en route* at Strichen, Banff (overnight), Cullen, Elgin and Forres (overnight)

Host (at Elgin): Bailie Robert Leslie, landlord of the Red Lion

From Slains Castle, which they left on the morning of 25th August, the travellers made their way to Strichen. Here they were shown the Druid's Temple by Alexander Fraser of Strichen, who afterwards entertained them to dinner with some of his neighbours. By nightfall they had reached Banff, and stayed at 'an indifferent inn', probably the Black Bull. They were on the road early next morning, and had breakfast at Cullen, possibly at the Horse's Head, where, according to Boswell, 'they set down dried haddocks broiled, along with our tea'. Boswell 'ate one; but Dr. Johnson was disgusted by the sight of them, so they were removed'. Proceeding on their way to Elgin, they passed Gordon Castle, and Fochabers, with its 'orchards well stored with apple trees'. In Elgin they 'saw the noble ruins of the Cathedral' and dined at the Red Lion, which had the only landlord in Scotland who wore ruffles. Boswell recorded that 'Bailie Leslie, at whose house we put up, gave us good fish, but beef collops and mutton chops which absolutely could not be eat. Dr. Johnson said this was the first time he had got a dinner in Scotland that he could not eat.' That afternoon they drove on to Forres, across the heath where Macbeth had traditionally met the three witches. 'We got to Forres at night,' wrote Boswell, 'and found an admirable inn,' which was kept by Lawson, a wine-cooper from London. They left Forres early the next day, 27th August, and had breakfast at Nairn.

Haddocks in Brown Sauce

Mrs. Dods called this 'an excellent Scotch Dish'; and in her recipe she added 'some mussels and a little wine' and '¼ hundred oysters'.

4 small haddocks	1½ oz. flour
1 pint (2½ cups) water	½ teaspoon mixed spice
1 onion, sliced	1 teaspoon mushroom ketchup
faggot of sweet herbs	juice of ½ lemon
strip of lemon peel	salt and pepper
1½ oz. butter	2 oz. prepared mussels (optional)

Clean the fish, remove the heads, trim the fins and tails, and remove the skins. Place these trimmings (except skins) in cold water with the onion, herbs and strip of lemon peel. Simmer for 30 minutes, and strain. Divide each fish into 2 or 3 neat pieces, and pass through seasoned flour. Melt the butter, and fry the fish until golden brown. Remove, and keep warm. Stir the flour into the remaining butter (adding extra, if necessary). Cook the roux until golden brown. Gradually stir in the fish stock, add spice, mushroom ketchup, juice of ½ lemon, and salt and pepper. Stir to the boil, and simmer for 2–3 minutes. The sauce should be thick and spicy. Check the seasoning. Carefully add the haddock pieces, simmer *very gently* for about 5 minutes. Add the mussels (if used), and heat thoroughly. Serve on a hot ashet. Serves 4.

Cullen Skink

A fish soup.

1 Finnan haddock, about 1¼ lb.	8 oz. (2 cups) mashed potatoes
1 medium onion, sliced	salt and pepper
1 pint (2½ cups) milk	2 oz. (¼ cup) butter

Skin the smoked haddock, cut into two, place in a saucepan with the onion, and just cover with cold water. Bring slowly to the boil, and simmer for 10–15 minutes. Remove the fish with a slice, remove all the bones, and flake the fish. Return the bones to the fish stock, cover, simmer for 30 minutes and strain. Bring the milk to the boil, add strained stock, flaked fish, pepper and a little salt if necessary. Gradually add the mashed potatoes, and mix thoroughly to a *purée* consistency. Gradually stir in the butter, to enrich. Reheat without boiling. Serve hot. Serves 3–4.

Cawdor Castle, by Beattie
The seat of the Campbells, Earls of Cawdor, visited by Johnson and Boswell on
27th August 1773

27th–28th August   Nairn to Cawdor

Hosts: Rev. Kenneth Macaulay, Minister of Cawdor, and his wife Penelope Macleod

From Nairn, Johnson and Boswell moved on to Cawdor to stay with Kenneth Macaulay, an 'exceedingly hospitable' minister who had 'a remarkably good manse ... very decently furnished'. After dinner their host showed them nearby Cawdor Castle, the seat of the absent Earl of Cawdor, a Campbell. 'The old tower', wrote Boswell, 'must be of great antiquity. There is a drawbridge, what has been a moat, and an ancient court.' That evening they enjoyed the company of Rev. Alexander Grant of Daviot, who also stayed overnight; and their host helped Boswell to trace out on a map their route 'from Inverness by Fort Augustus to Glenelg, Skye, Mull, Icolmkill, Lorne, and Inveraray,' where their host's brother, John Macaulay, was minister. Before leaving the next day, Johnson promised Mrs. Macaulay to help her son enter Oxford University, for which kindness she 'was wisely and truly grateful'. During conversation, Johnson remarked on the Scottish practice of saying grace at breakfast, which he found odd, but he 'allowed the peculiar merit of breakfast in Scotland'. Indeed, in a general observation, Johnson admitted that breakfast was 'a meal in which the Scots, whether of the lowlands or mountains, must be confessed to excel us. The tea and coffee are accompanied not only with butter, but with honey, conserves, and marmalades.' His omission of oatcakes, a traditional Scottish breakfast food, was perhaps deliberate, on account of the famous definition he had given in his *Dictionary* for 'Oats': 'a grain which in England is generally given to horses, but in Scotland supports the people'.

Oatcakes

Traditionally, oatcakes are mixed with a *spurtle* or porridge-stick, then cooked on a girdle or griddle over a peat fire, and finished on a toasting-stone in front of the open hearth. A large oatcake is called a Bannock, and these cut into quarters are known as Farls.

4 oz. (1 cup) medium or fine oatmeal	1 rounded tablespoon of dripping
½ level teaspoon of salt	*or* bacon fat, melted
good pinch bicarbonate of soda	3–4 tablespoons boiling water

Place the oatmeal, salt and bicarbonate of soda in a bowl. Make a well, pour in the melted fat and boiling water, and mix to a fairly stiff consistency. Turn onto a board, well-sprinkled with fine oatmeal. Knead well, adding more oatmeal if the dough shows signs of sticking. Form into a round, flatten with the knuckles, roll out fairly thinly to a circle and cut with a saucepan-lid. Rub with a little more oatmeal and cut into four. Place on a heated girdle, or in a thick-bottomed frying-pan, sprinkled with a little flour. Cook for about 5 minutes, until the edges curl. Place to crisp for a few minutes in a moderate oven, or under a low grill. It is advisable to make one bannock at a time, as the mixture dries out very quickly, and becomes difficult to handle.

Baps

8 oz. (2 cups) plain 'strong' flour	1 tablespoon lard
1 level teaspoon sugar	½ oz. fresh yeast
½ level teaspoon salt	¼ pint (approx. ⅔ cup) lukewarm milk

Sieve the flour, sugar, and salt into a warm bowl. Rub in the lard. Dissolve the yeast in the milk, and add to the flour. Knead until smooth, adding a little more flour if the dough is sticky. Cover, and leave in a warm place for about 45 minutes, until the dough has doubled in size. Turn onto a floured board, and knead lightly. Divide into eight, and mould into flat ovals. Place on a floured baking-tray. Cover, and leave in a warm place for about 15–20 minutes. Dust with flour, and bake in a preheated hot oven, Gas No. 7: 425°F., for about 15 minutes. Serve hot.

View of Fort George and the Town of Inverness, by Paul Sandby
Fort George (or Inverness Castle) before it was blown up in 1746. Johnson and
Boswell saw only the ruins. They also visited the other Fort George at
Ardersier, near Inverness.

28th August Cawdor to Inverness, stopping *en route* at Fort George

Hosts (at Fort George): Colonel Sir Eyre Coote, K.B., Lt.-Governor of Fort George, and his wife Susanna Hutchison, Lady Coote

On the morning of 28th August, Johnson and Boswell made the short journey from Cawdor to Fort George. With a letter from Valentine White, the Welsh factor to the Earl of Cawdor, the travellers introduced themselves to George Fern, the master of the stores, who, in turn, introduced them to Major John Brewse of the Engineers. Fern and Brewse took them immediately to meet Sir Eyre Coote, the veteran of many campaigns in India, who asked them 'to eat a bit of mutton with him'. Before dinner they were shown the fort. 'At three', wrote Boswell, 'the drum beat for dinner. I, for a little while, fancied myself a military man, and it pleased me. We went to Sir Eyre Coote's, at the Governor's house, and found him a most gentleman-like man. His lady is a very agreeable woman, with an uncommonly mild and sweet tone of voice. ... We had a dinner of two complete courses, variety of wines, and the regimental band of music playing in the square before the windows.' Johnson said: 'I shall always remember this fort with gratitude.' They left between six and seven in the evening, and went the short distance to the town of Inverness, where they stayed at Mackenzie's Inn. James Keith, the Collector of Excise at Inverness, whom Boswell had known at Ayr, had seen them at the fort, and called on them at the inn in the evening and, wrote Boswell, 'engaged us to dine with him next day, promising to breakfast with us'.

Roast Saddle of Mutton

The influence of the 'Auld Alliance' between Scotland and France is reflected in many eighteenth-century Scottish recipes. 'To Roast a Saddle of Mutton the French Way,' wrote Mrs. Cleland, 'chuse a fine fat Saddle or two Loins'. She then gave the following stuffing: 'sweet herbs, parsley, pepper, bay salt, mace, ham, onions, truffles, morels.' The saddle is an ideal joint for a large family party. For a smaller gathering the cutlet piece (best end), which consists of 6 bones, is more practical. Choice of lamb or mutton is, of course, a matter of taste and availability.

1 short saddle lamb or mutton, 4–6 lb.	*for the stuffing*
	4 oz. white breadcrumbs
or 1 cutlet piece (best end), 2 lb.	4 oz. (½ cup) butter
	2 oz. chopped ham
salt and mill pepper	2 oz. chopped mushrooms
2–4 oz. dripping	½ small onion, finely chopped
¾ pint (2 cups) stock for gravy	chopped thyme, rosemary, parsley
	(only ½ the above for cutlet piece)

Ask the butcher to prepare the saddle for roasting, or, if cutlet piece is used, to remove the chine bone. Lightly score the fat with a knife, rub well with salt and milled pepper. Place dripping on top, and roast in a fairly hot oven, Gas No. 5 : 375°F., allowing 20 minutes to each pound, and 20 minutes over.

THE STUFFING Prepare the breadcrumbs. Melt the butter in a small pan, add the chopped ham, mushroom and onion. Cook for 1 minute; do not colour. Stir in the herbs, salt and pepper, and sufficient crumbs to form a spreading consistency (do not make too dry, or it will be difficult to spread).

TO COMPLETE 20 minutes before the end of the cooking time, remove the meat. Spread on the stuffing, return to the oven, and complete the cooking. Remove the meat onto a hot ashet, and leave in a warm place while the gravy is made. Drain off the fat from the roasting-tin, add stock, and simmer with the juices. Add salt and pepper, and strain into a sauce-boat. A saddle is carved lengthwise on either side of the backbone. A cutlet piece is divided between the bones. Serve mint sauce with lamb, and rowan or redcurrant jelly (see p. 65) with mutton.

Spinning with the Distaff, by McIan
The plaids noticed by Johnson were made from wool spun in the homes of
Highland women. Outside the cottage the artist has shown a typical 'hake', on
which fish were hung to dry.

28th–30th August   In Inverness, and the start of the tour on horseback

Host: Kenneth Mackenzie, landlord of The Horns in Inverness, the former town house of the family of Forbes of Culloden

After attending the English Church with James Keith on the morning of 29th August, the travellers walked to Inverness quay. Here they met the miniature painter James Alves, whom Boswell had not seen since they were in Rome in 1765. They then went to view Inverness Castle, which Boswell wrongly assumed was 'Macbeth's Castle', before dining with James Keith. Mrs. Keith was rather too attentive to Johnson, 'asking him many questions about his drinking only water'. Johnson rebuked her, and implied that she was ill-bred by saying to Boswell: 'You may remember that Lady Erroll took no notice of this.' In the evening James Keith, and Rev. Alexander Grant, whom they had met at Cawdor Manse, were their guests for dinner at Mackenzie's inn,

and they had 'roasted kid'. The next morning, after two nights with Mackenzie, they prepared for the arduous part of their tour. Writing about Inverness, Johnson said: 'Here the appearance of life began to alter. I had seen a few women with plaids at Aberdeen, but at Inverness the Highland manners are common. . . . We were now to bid farewell to the luxury of travelling, and to enter a country upon which, perhaps, no wheel has ever rolled. . . . At Inverness we procured three horses for ourselves and a servant, and one more for our baggage. . . . We mounted our steeds on the thirtieth of August, and directed our guides to conduct us to Fort Augustus.'

As roasted kid is rarely, if ever, eaten today, and as the travellers mentioned no other dishes while they were in Inverness, the recipes chosen for this page are for biscuits, which have always been popular in Scotland. 'To make a Spunge Bisket,' wrote Mrs. McLintock, 'take 15 Eggs, keep out 2 Whites, take a lib. of fine Sugar, beat them till they be thick and white, and take 3 Quarters of a lib. of Flour, and the Grate of 2 Lemons, mix them together, then put them in the Pans, and send them to the Oven.'

Chocolate Biscuits

4 oz. (1 cup) self-raising flour	4 oz. ($\frac{1}{2}$ cup) granulated sugar
1 oz. rice flour, or ground rice	4 oz. ($\frac{1}{2}$ cup) margarine
1 oz. cocoa powder	

Sieve the dry ingredients into a bowl. Add the sugar and margarine, and knead together until smooth. Roll the mixture into balls the

size of a walnut, and place them apart on a greased baking-tray. Flatten gently with the back of a fork. Bake in the middle of a pre-heated moderate oven, Gas No. 4: 350°F., for 15–20 minutes. Cool on a wire rack. Makes 20–24 biscuits.

Crispy Biscuits

4 oz. (1 cup) self-raising flour	1 oz. hazel nuts, chopped
1$\frac{1}{2}$ oz. margarine	$\frac{1}{2}$ egg, beaten
4 oz. ($\frac{3}{4}$ cup) soft brown sugar	

Sieve the flour into a bowl. Add the margarine, and rub in until the mixture resembles breadcrumbs. Stir in the sugar and hazel nuts. Bind with the egg to a stiff dough. Roll it on a lightly-floured board into a sausage shape, about 1$\frac{1}{2}$ inches in diameter. Cut into $\frac{1}{4}$-inch slices, and place apart on a greased baking-tray. Bake in the middle of a pre-heated moderate oven, Gas No. 4: 350°F., for 15–20 minutes. Cool on a wire rack. Makes 16–18 biscuits.

A Highland Cottage, artist unknown, from Dr. Isabel F. Grant's collection
The interior of a typical eighteenth-century Highland cottage; probably similar
to the Frasers' home on the banks of Loch Ness which the travellers visited.

30th August In the Great Glen, travelling along the east bank of Loch Ness

Hosts: The Fraser Family, goatherds on Loch Ness side, tenants of William Fraser of Balnain

'Loch Ness', wrote Johnson, 'is about twenty-four miles long. . . . Its water is remarkably clear and pleasant, and is imagined by the natives to be medicinal. . . . Part of it is bordered with low trees, from which our guides gathered nuts.' He made no mention of the legendary Loch Ness Monster, and nor did his friend. 'When we had advanced a good way by the side of Loch Ness,' said Boswell, 'I perceived a little hut, with an old-looking woman at the door. . . . It was a wretched little hovel of earth only, I think, and for a window had only a small hole, which was stopped with a piece of turf, that was taken out occasionally to let in light. In the middle of the room was a fire of peat, the smoke going out at a hole in the roof. She had a pot upon it, with goat's flesh boiling. . . . The woman's name was Fraser; so was her husband's. He was a man of eighty. . . . They had five children, the eldest only thirteen. Two were gone to Inverness to buy meal; the rest were looking after the goats. This contented family had four stacks of barley . . . [and] a few fowls. We were informed that they lived all the spring without meal, upon milk and curds and whey alone. What they get for their goats, kids, and fowls, maintains them during the rest of the year. She asked us to sit down and take a dram. . . . She asked for snuff. It is her luxury, and she uses a great deal. We had none; but gave her sixpence a piece.' From the goatherds' shanty the travellers moved on to Foyers and Boleskine. 'We came to dinner,' wrote Boswell, 'to a public house called the General's Hut. . . . We had mutton-chops, a broiled chicken, and bacon and eggs, and a bottle of Malaga.' From the public house, which was named after General George Wade, the great military road-builder, they continued on their way through 'a good deal of mountainous country' to Fort Augustus.

Chicken Stovies

Also called Stoved Chicken.

1 chicken, 2½ lb.	8 oz. peeled onions
1 pint stock (2½ cups), made from the carcase and giblets	salt and pepper
1½ lb. peeled potatoes	1 tablespoon butter
	chopped parsley

Joint the chicken by removing the legs from the carcase, and cut each at the joint into two. Remove the wings with some of the breast meat. Finally, remove the breast, and divide into two. This gives 8 pieces in all. Crush the carcase, and simmer gently with the giblets to make stock. Slice the potatoes about ¼ inch thick, and halve and finely slice the onions. Sprinkle the chicken joints with salt and pepper. Melt the butter in a heavy casserole, put in the joints, and seal the outsides. (It may be necessary to seal the chicken joints in a frying-pan, if the right type of casserole is not available.) Place a layer of sliced potato, then onion, then chicken joints, and a few shavings of butter. Season well, and continue until all the ingredients are used, finishing with a layer of potato. Barely cover with chicken stock, and cover the casserole with a tight-fitting lid. Place in a slow oven, Gas No. 2: 300°F., for 1½–2 hours, adding a little more stock, if necessary. Sprinkle liberally with parsley before serving. If preferred, chicken stovies can be cooked in a heavy-based pan, and allowed to simmer on top of the stove for 1½ hours. Serves 4.

Mutton or lamb cutlets or chops can be used instead of chicken, and prepared in the same way.

Fort Augustus, by Thomas Sandby
Built by General Wade in 1730 to keep the Highlanders under control

30th–31st August   At Fort Augustus, Inverness-shire

Host: Captain Alexander Trapaud, Lt.-Governor of Fort Augustus

'We did not arrive at Fort Augustus', wrote Johnson, 'till it was late. Mr. Boswell, between his father's merit and his own, is sure of a reception wherever he comes. ... Trapaud, the governor, treated us with that courtesy which is so closely connected with the military character. He came out to meet us beyond the gates, and apologized that, at so late an hour, the rules of a garrison suffered him to give us entrance only at the postern.' Boswell, who had sent his servant Joseph ahead to inform his old acquaintance Captain Trapaud of their visit, was pleased to find inside the fort 'a neat well-furnished house with prints'. Trapaud, who was born in Ireland of French parents, gave the travellers a good supper of 'fricassee of moor-fowl'. Mrs. Trapaud, her daughter Mary, and the latter's husband, Captain Timothy Newmarch, were 'all most obliging and polite'; Captain Trapaud had 'excellent animal spirits'; and the travellers passed 'a very agreeable evening'. Before breakfast on the following day, 31st August, Johnson and Boswell viewed the fort. 'The Governor', said Boswell, 'has a very good garden. We looked at it and all the rest of the fort. ... We also looked at the galley or sloop belonging to the fort, which sails upon the Loch [Ness], and brings what is wanted for the garrison.'

Fricassée of Pheasant, Chicken, or Rabbit

Adapted from Mrs. McLintock's recipe for 'A Frigacy of Rabbets or Chickens', which she garnished with oysters, capers, and cucumber.

1 young pheasant *or* chicken, *or* young skinned rabbit	2 oz. (¼ cup) butter
1 onion	1 heaped tablespoon flour
faggot of herbs	salt and pepper
1 carrot	⅛ pint (⅓ cup) cream
1½ pints water	1 egg yolk
pinch of mace	juice of ½ lemon
	chopped parsley

Joint the pheasant, chicken, or skinned rabbit. Remove the skins (if birds are used). Crush the carcase, and place with trimmings in a pan. Add the onion, herbs, carrot, water, and mace. Simmer gently for 1 hour, and strain. Melt the butter in a pan, add the joints, and seal the outsides, without colouring. Stir in the flour, and cook gently for 1 minute. Gradually stir in 1 pint of the strained stock, and, stirring, bring to the boil. Add the salt and pepper, cover, and leave to simmer for 1 hour, or until cooked, stirring occasionally. Mix together the cream and egg yolk, and carefully stir this mixture into the sauce while off the heat. Return, and reheat slowly without boiling. Add a little lemon juice, and check the seasoning. Sprinkle with chopped parsley, or garnish (as Mrs. McLintock suggested) with capers and pickled cucumbers or gherkins. Serves 4.

SCOTTISH WEIGHTS AND MEASURES   As these are given in this book in quotations from eighteenth-century recipes, a note of their English equivalents is required. In 1773 Mrs. Susanna Maciver wrote: '1 Scotch Pint is equal to 4 English Pints; 1 Scotch Chopin to 2 English Pints; 1 Scotch Mutchkin to one English Pint; 1 Scotch half-Mutchkin to a half-Pint English.' She could have added that 2 Scotch Pints were treated as one English Gallon, although they were not exactly equal. An English Gallon was slightly more than the accepted Scottish equivalent. The term 'Chopin' was more often given as 'Choppin', but both were accepted spellings.

31st August–1st September   Fort Augustus to Anoch in Glenmoriston

Host: James Macqueen, landlord of the Anoch Inn, Glenmoriston

At midday on 31st August, Johnson and Boswell left Fort Augustus, and travelled eleven miles to Macqueen's Inn at Anoch in Glenmoriston. 'The house here', wrote Boswell, 'was built of thick turfs, and thatched with thinner turfs and heath. . . . The side-walls were *wainscotted*, as Dr. Johnson said, with wicker, very neatly plaited. Our landlord had made the whole with his own hands.' Boswell continued: 'We had a broiled chicken, mutton collops or chops, mutton sausage, and eggs, of which Dr. Johnson eat five and nothing else. I eat four, some chicken and some sausage, and drank some rum and water and sugar. Joseph had lemons for Dr. Johnson, so he had lemonade. . . . We had tea in the afternoon, and our landlord's daughter, a modest civil girl, very neatly dressed, made it for us. She told us, she had been a year at Inverness, and learnt reading and writing, sewing, knotting, working lace, and pastry.' That night the travellers slept in one of the inn's three rooms. 'There were two beds in the room,' said Boswell, 'and a woman's gown was hung on a rope to make a curtain of separation between them. . . . We had much hesitation whether to undress, or lie down with our clothes on. . . . Dr. Johnson fell asleep immediately. I was not so fortunate. . . . I fancied myself bit by innumerable vermin under the clothes; and that a spider was travelling from the *wainscot* towards my mouth.' After breakfast the next morning, 1st September, Macqueen went some way with the travellers to set them on their route.

Lemonade

Mrs. Robertson wrote: 'Take two Scotch pints of spring water and two pounds of loaf sugar, and boil them softly for three quarter of an hour; when the liquor is near cold put to it the juice of twelve lemons; then toast a piece of brown bread and spread it with barm, and put it to the liquor; let it stand two days, then bottle it; if you think it not sweet enough, put a lump of sugar in each bottle.' Barm is the froth on fermenting malt liquor.

Gingerbread

Miss Macqueen probably learned to make this at her pastry lessons in Inverness. The following is adapted from Mrs. McLintock's recipe for Ginger Cake, to which she added ½ oz. caraway seeds.

Mrs. Robertson's alternative was to add chopped mixed peel.

8 oz. (2 cups) plain flour	8 oz. (¾ cup) black treacle
3–4 level teaspoons ground ginger	¼ pint (⅔ cup) milk
1 oz. fine oatmeal	1 egg
4 oz. (½ cup) margarine or lard	½ level teaspoon bicarbonate
4 oz. (¾ cup) soft brown sugar	of soda

Sieve the flour and ginger into a bowl. Add the oatmeal. Place the margarine or lard, sugar, treacle, and milk into a saucepan. Melt slowly, without overheating. Break the egg, and lightly beat. Dissolve the bicarbonate of soda in the cooled mixture. Pour onto the flour with the egg, and beat until smooth. Pour into a 7-inch square cake-tin, previously lined with greased paper. Bake in the middle of a pre-heated very moderate oven, Gas No. 3: 325°F., for 1¼–1½ hours. Cool on a wire rack. Wrap in foil or in a polythene bag, and store for a few days in an airtight tin before cutting.

Lodging at Macqueen's, by Rowlandson
Boswell trying to get to sleep in the squalid bedroom at Macqueen's Inn. Two rats gnaw at Boswell's wig, and a spider descends towards his head.

1st–2nd September   Glenmoriston to Glenelg, by way of Auchnashiel and Mam Rattachan

Host: Donald Munro, landlord of the Inn at Glenelg

On parting from Macqueen, the travellers passed through Glen Shiel, which had 'prodigious mountains on each side', to Auchnashiel. Here, 'we sat down', wrote Boswell, 'on a green turf seat at the end of a house, and they brought us out two wooden dishes of milk, which we tasted. One of them was frothed like a sillabub. I saw a woman preparing it with such a stick as is used for chocolate, and in the same manner. ... Dr. Johnson was much refreshed by this repast.' They then rode on to the steep mountain called Mam Rattachan, where Johnson was much fatigued by the climb. On the far side of it, Boswell decided to go ahead to arrange accommodation for the night, and Johnson, thinking he was being left behind, lost his temper. Boswell, to save his friend further distress, stayed with him until they reached Glenelg. 'At last', wrote Johnson, 'we came on an inn', which belonged to a Munro from Fort Augustus, but, noted Boswell, 'they had no bread, no eggs, no wine, no spirits but whisky, no sugar but brown grown black. They prepared some mutton chops, but we would not have them. They killed two hens. I made Joseph broil me a bit of one till it was black, and I tasted it. Dr. Johnson would have nothing but a bit of bread ... and some lemonade.' They were sent, however, a bottle of 'excellent rum' by John Murchison, the factor of Glenelg, whose servant Ewen Campbell had met them on the road during the day. Johnson was much impressed by this 'very eminent proof of Highland hospitality'. The travellers passed a miserable night trying to sleep on beds of hay they made for themselves on the floor of the inn. On rising, they discussed their quarrel on the previous day, and enjoyed a reconciliation.

Sillabubs

To make 'Solid Sillabubs,' Mrs. Cleland said: 'Take a Chopin of very thick Cream, put into it three Gills of Malaga, the Grate of a Lemon, the juice of two bitter Oranges, and sweeten it to your Taste; beat it well together for a Quarter of an Hour, then skim it with a Spoon, and put it in Glasses.'

2 lemons	4 tablespoons brandy ⎱ *or* port wine
6 oz. (¾ cup) caster (fine) sugar	4 tablespoons sherry ⎰
	1 pint double cream

Wash and thinly peel the lemons. Squeeze the juice into a bowl. Add the lemon peel, and leave to stand for 2 hours. Strain onto the caster sugar. Add the brandy and sherry (or port, if preferred), and stir well. Pour on the double cream, and whisk until thick. Pour into glasses. Serves 8.

Oon

From Martin Martin's *A Description of the Western Islands of Scotland* (published in 1703, 2nd edition 1716), which Johnson and Boswell took with them on their tour.

'Oon, which in *English* signifies Froth, is made in the following manner: A quantity of Milk or Whey is boil'd in a Pot, and then it is wrought up to the mouth of the Pot with a long stick of Wood, having a Cross at the lower-end; it is turn'd about like the Stick for making Chocolate: and being thus made it is supp'd with Spoons. It is made up five or six times, in the same manner, and the last is always reckon'd best.'

The Reconciliation, by Rowlandson
Dr. Johnson had thought that Boswell was deserting him on the road to Glenelg, and had lost his temper. Here, at Glenelg inn, the following morning, the friends are reconciled.

2nd–6th September Glenelg to Armadale in the Isle of Skye

Host: Sir Alexander Macdonald of Sleat, Bt. (later Lord Macdonald of Sleat), and his wife Elizabeth Diana Bosville, Lady Macdonald of Sleat

On the morning of 2nd September, the travellers dismissed their Highland guides at Glenelg, and took a boat to Skye. So began their tour of the Hebrides. 'We landed at Armadale,' wrote Johnson, 'where we were met on the sands by Sir Alexander Macdonald, who was at that time there with his lady, preparing to leave the island and reside at Edinburgh. ... As we sat at Sir Alexander's table, we were entertained according to the ancient usage of the North, with the melody of the bagpipe.' Although the travellers stayed four nights with Sir Alexander, and were well treated, Boswell was far from complimentary about his distinguished host, who as *Macdonald of the Isles* held the most revered title in the Highlands. Remarking on the first meal they had at Armadale, Boswell wrote: 'We had an ill-dressed dinner, Sir Alexander not having a cook of any kind from Edinburgh. I alone drank port wine. No claret appeared. We had indeed mountain [Malaga wine] and Frontignac and Scotch porter. But except

what I did myself, there was no hospitable convivial intercourse, no ringing of glasses.' Sir Alexander 'stuck his fork into a liver pudding. ... I took care to act as he ought to have done. There was no wheat-loaf, but only a kind of bannock or cake, raw in the heart, as it was so thick. Sir Alexander himself drank punch ... which he distributed to those men who were accustomed even in their own houses to much better. He gave it with a pewter dividing-spoon which had served the broth. At tea there were few cups and no tea-tongs nor a supernumerary tea-spoon, so we used our fingers.' When they left on 6th September, Sir Alexander gave the travellers the use of his own horses. He was therefore angry, when Boswell produced the first edition of his *Tour* in 1785, to find that it contained scornful comments about himself and his wife. This nearly led to a duel, and Boswell was careful to placate Macdonald when he produced the second edition of his work.

Haggis (or Scotch Liver Pudding)

'A Haggis', wrote John Caird, 'is generally made with a sheep's draught, or pluck; wash and clean it well by slitting all the pipes and heart; parboil, then mince it small; boil the liver well and grate the half of it; shred small from ten ounces to a pound of suet, according to the size of the meat, a few onions, and half a pound of oatmeal; mix it well together, and season it with mixed spices, pepper and salt to your taste. Have ready the Haggis bag, perfectly sweet and clean, pour into the compound a quart (choppin) of good gravy, mix it up and fill the bag, press out all the air before you sew it up. If the bag is thin, tie in a cloth to prevent its bursting. A pretty large one requires about two hours boiling.'

Pot Haggis, with Neep Purry

Mrs. Dods put a little ginger in her Neep Purry, which is the Scottish term for mashed turnips.

8 oz. sheep's liver	2 oz. ($\frac{1}{2}$ cup) fine oatmeal
2 medium onions	salt and pepper
2 oz. ($\frac{1}{2}$ cup) beef suet	pinch of Cayenne or Jamaica pepper

Place the liver in a small saucepan, cover with water, and simmer gently for 30 minutes. Keep the stock. Mince the liver. Finely chop the onions, and the suet (if bought unprepared), and toast the oatmeal in the oven for about 10 minutes. Mix all the ingredients together with the seasoning and with sufficient stock to moisten well (about $\frac{1}{2}$ pint). Place in a well-greased medium-sized basin. Cover with foil or greased paper, and steam for 2–$2\frac{1}{2}$ hours. Remove, stand for a few minutes, and turn out onto a hot ashet. Serve with mashed potatoes and neep purry. Serves 3–4.

Revising for the Second Edition, by Rowlandson
Boswell cringes before Sir Alexander Macdonald, who points to some observations in the First Edition of Boswell's *Tour* which had angered him. Boswell made sure that they were omitted in the Second Edition.

The Coolin, taken from Loch Slapin, by Daniell
Johnson and Boswell saw the Cuillin (or Coolin) Hills of Skye on many
occasions when they were on the island

6th–8th September   Armadale to Coirechatachan (or Corrie), Isle of Skye

Hosts: Lachlan Mackinnon of Corrie, and his third wife Anne Macdonald of Kingsburgh

While at Armadale, the travellers received an invitation to stay on the Isle of Raasay. *En route* they stayed for two nights with Mackinnon of Corrie, near Broadford in Skye. 'The house', wrote Boswell, 'was of two storeys. We were carried into a low parlour, with a carpet on the floor, which we had not seen at Armadale. We had tea in good order, a *trea*, silver tea-pot, silver sugar-dish and tongs, silver tea-spoons enough. Our landlord's father had found a treasure of old silver coins, and of these he had made his plate. . . . Mrs. Mackinnon was a decent well-behaved old gentle-woman in a black silk gown. . . . We had for supper a large dish of minced beef collops, a large dish of fricassée of fowl, I believe a dish called fried [or friar's] chicken or something like it, a dish of ham or tongue, some excellent haddocks, some herrings, a large bowl of rich milk, frothed, as good a bread-pudding as I ever tasted, full of raisins and lemon or orange peel, and sillabubs made with port wine and in sillabub glasses.' On the next day, 7th September, Captain John Macdonald of Breakish (soon to leave for Canada) came to dinner. 'We had', said Boswell, 'a good plentiful one: roast mutton, a chicken-pie, and I forget how many good dishes. After it we had several Erse [Gaelic] songs, and a bowl of stout punch.' That evening, some visiting guests 'assembled round a good peat fire, and drank two or three bottles of porter' followed by an 'excellent supper, and many lively Erse songs after it'. After breakfast, on 8th September, the travellers left Corrie and went to the nearby shore to find their boat for Raasay.

Friar's Chicken

Mrs. Dods gave her recipe for this dish as follows: 'Make a clear stock of veal, mutton shanks, or trimmings of fowl. Strain this into a very nice saucepan, and put a fine white chicken cut down. Season with pepper, salt, mace, and shred parsley. Thicken with the yolks of two eggs, and take care not to curdle.' The success of this dish depends on using stock with a good 'body' and flavour.

1 chicken, 2½ lb.	blade of mace
2 lb. veal bones (if available)	2 egg yolks
4 pints water	1 tablespoon chopped parsley
salt and pepper	1 oz. butter

Joint the chicken by removing the legs and cutting into two. Remove the winglets. Remove the breast and divide. Remove the skin from the joints. Use all the carcase, trimmings, skin, and veal bones (if obtainable). Cover with cold water, bring to the boil, skim well, and simmer for 2 hours. Strain the stock into a clean pan. Bring to the boil, add the seasoned chicken joints and mace, and simmer gently until the chicken is cooked; skim if necessary. Remove the mace. Pour a little of the warm stock onto the egg yolks, stir well and, stirring gradually, add to the broth. Reheat, but do not boil. Toss in 1 oz. butter, add the parsley, and check the seasoning. Serves 4–6.

Drop Scones (for High Tea)

8 oz. (2 cups) plain flour	1 level tablespoon caster sugar
1 level teaspoon cream of tartar	1 level tablespoon golden syrup
½ level teaspoon bicarbonate of soda	1 egg
pinch of salt	approx. ¼ pint of milk

Sieve the flour, raising agents, and salt into a bowl. Add the sugar. Beat in the syrup, the egg and milk to form a smooth, fairly thick batter. Have ready a heated, lightly-greased girdle or thick frying-pan. Drop in desertspoonfuls of the mixture, and cook over a moderate heat until bubbles appear all over. Turn, and cook on the other side. Remove, and place in a cloth until ready for use. Serve them spread with butter and heather honey, or bramble jelly (see p. 65). Makes 15 scones.

From the Isle of Raasay, looking westward, by Daniell
Showing Raasay House, as it was when Johnson and Boswell stayed there

8th–9th September Corrie, Isle of Skye, to the Isle of Raasay

Hosts: John Macleod of Raasay, and his wife Jane Macqueen, Lady Raasay

From Skye, the travellers crossed to the Isle of Raasay in the laird's 'carriage, which was a good strong open boat made in Norway'. Boswell thought that the approach to Raasay was 'very pleasing' with its 'beautiful bay' and the 'good family mansion'; and the 'boatmen sang with great spirits' as they rowed across the water. They were treated well by Macleod of Raasay, one of the lairds who had helped Bonnie Prince Charlie escape from Scotland after the disastrous failure of the Jacobite rising at the Battle of Culloden in 1746. 'Our reception', wrote Johnson, 'exceeded our expectations. We found nothing but civility, elegance, and plenty. ... The family of Raasay consists of the laird, the lady, three sons, and ten daughters. For the sons there is a tutor in the house, and the lady is said to be very skilful and diligent in the education of her girls. More gentleness of manners, or a more pleasing appearance of domestic society, is not found in the most polished countries.' Boswell agreed with this patronizing comment. 'We found here', he said, 'coffee and tea in genteel order upon the table, as it was past six when we arrived: diet loaf, marmalade of oranges, currant jelly; some elegantly bound books on a large table, in short, all the marks of an improved life. We had a dram of excellent brandy. ... On a sideboard was served up directly, for us who had come off the sea, mutton-chops and tarts, with porter, claret, mountain, and punch. Then we had coffee and tea. In a little, a fiddler appeared, and a little ball began. ... We had a company of thirty at supper, and all was good humour and gaiety. Many songs were sung. ... The glass circulated briskly, but nobody was asked to drink more than he cared to, and there was no intemperance.'

Diet Loaf

This is a very light sponge cake, flavoured with spices and caraway seeds or lemon. When baked, the top can be sprinkled with icing sugar; or the sponge can be split and filled with whipped cream and fresh fruit, such as strawberries or raspberries. Mrs. McLintock gave the following recipe: 'Take 9 Eggs, beat them with 3 Quarters of a lib. of Sugar, till they be thick and white, take 2 Drop of Cinnamon, 2 Drop of Nutmeg, 2 Drop of Cloves, a Quarter of an Ounce of Carvey [Caraway]-Seed, 3 Quarters of a lib. of Flour, mix all together, and put in your Frame, and send it to the Oven.'

3 large eggs	grated rind of $\frac{1}{2}$ lemon
4 oz. ($\frac{1}{2}$ cup) caster (fine) sugar	*or* 1 level teaspoon caraway
3 oz. ($\frac{3}{4}$ cup) plain flour	seeds
1 level teaspoon mixed spice	icing sugar, for dusting

Place the eggs and sugar in a bowl. Place this over a pan of hot water and whisk for about 10 minutes until very light and frothy (or use an electric mixer, until very light and frothy). Remove the bowl from the heat, and whisk until cool, so that the whisk leaves a 'trail' when lifted. Sieve the flour and spices onto a plate. Beat in the lemon or caraway seeds. Using a metal spoon, cut and fold the flour into the mixture. Have ready an 8 inch deep cake-tin, which has been greased and the bottom lined with a round of paper. Dust the inside of the tin with a mixture of flour and sugar. Pour in the sponge mixture. Bake on the middle shelf of a pre-heated moderate oven, Gas No. 4: 350°F., for 20 minutes, or until the mixture shrinks away from the side of the tin. Remove from the oven, leave to stand for a few minutes, and turn onto a wire rack. Dust with icing sugar, or split when cold and fill with whipped cream and crushed fruit.

9th–12th September   At Raasay House on the Isle of Raasay

Hosts: John Macleod of Raasay, and his wife Jane Macqueen, Lady Raasay

On the first morning on Raasay, 'I had', wrote Boswell, 'goat's whey brought to my bedside. Then [I] rose and partook of an excellent breakfast: as good chocolate as I ever tasted, tea, bread and butter, marmalade and jelly. There was no loaf-bread, but very good *scones*, or cakes of flour baked with butter. There was a plate of butter and curd mixed, which they call *gruitheam*; cakes of what is called *graddaned* meal, that is, meal burnt with straw in place of being threshed and kiln-dried.... There was also barley bannocks of this year's meal, and—what I cannot help disliking to have at breakfast—cheese. It is the custom over all the Highlands to have it; and it often smells very strong.' Leaving Johnson indoors, Boswell went for a walk with the laird and 'had a very solid, easy, feudal chat' and then, with Alexander Macleod of Muiravonside, the former A.D.C. to Bonnie Prince Charlie, he went to shoot black cock, but this was spoiled by rain. The next day Boswell went off with some of the laird's other guests for an outing, again without Johnson, who was 'unable to take so hardy a walk'. This took Boswell and his companions to the top of Dun-Can, the highest mountain, where, said Boswell, 'we sat down, eat cold mutton and bread and cheese and drank brandy and punch.... Then we danced a reel'. The travellers spent two more days with their delightful hosts. Johnson observed: 'This is truly the patriarchal life. This is what we came to find.... If one had a mind to retire to study for a summer, it would be a fine place.' Johnson was especially impressed by the laird's children, particularly Flora Macleod, the future Countess of Loudoun. 'They were', he told Boswell, 'the best-bred children he ever saw; that he did not believe there was such another family between here and London.... They dance every night all the year round. There seemed to be no jealousy, no discontent among them.'

Oven Scones

Traditionally, the various bannocks, oatcakes, and scones, were baked on a griddle. In 1773 wheat flour was little used in the Highlands, and most of the bannocks were made of bere (or barley meal), oatmeal, or peasemeal.

Plain Scones

8 oz. (2 cups) plain flour	8 oz. (2 cups) self-raising
pinch of salt	flour
1 level teaspoon cream of tartar *or*	and
½ level teaspoon bicarbonate of	1 level teaspoon baking-
soda	powder
2 oz. (¼ cup) butter or margarine	
¼ pint (⅔ cup) milk, or buttermilk	

Sieve the flour, salt and raising agents into a bowl. Rub in fat until the mixture resembles breadcrumbs. Add the milk, and mix to a soft dough with the blade of a knife. Turn out onto a lightly-floured board. Divide into half, and roll out to 2 rounds, each ¾ inch thick. Mark each round into four, and place on a floured baking-tray. Brush with milk, and bake in a pre-heated hot oven, Gas No. 7: 425°F., for 10–12 minutes. If preferred, make into small rounds with a cutter, and bake in a hot oven for 10 minutes.

SWEET SCONES   Stir in 1 oz. caster sugar with the flour.

FRUIT SCONES   Stir in 1 oz. caster sugar and 1 oz. sultanas.

OATMEAL SCONES   Use 4 oz. fine oatmeal, and 4 oz. flour. Add 1 oz. caster sugar.

TREACLE SCONES   Warm 1 heaped tablespoon treacle, and mix with the milk. Add 1 level teaspoon of mixed spice.

WHOLEMEAL SCONES   Use 4 oz. wholemeal flour and 4 oz. flour. Add 1 oz. caster sugar.

The Dance on Dun-Can, by Rowlandson
Boswell performing a Highland Reel on the top of Dun-Can, the highest mountain on Raasay

12th–13th September   Raasay to Kingsburgh, Isle of Skye, stopping *en route* at Portree

Hosts: Allan Macdonald of Kingsburgh, and his wife Flora Macdonald of Milton

On 12th September the travellers went by boat from Raasay to Portree, the main town on Skye, where they had a meal at James Macdonald's inn. They then rode north to Kingsburgh House, to stay with Flora Macdonald, the great heroine of the 1745 rising, who was still called 'Miss Flora' although she was married to a fellow-clansman, Allan Macdonald, the laird of Kingsburgh. 'He was', wrote Boswell, 'completely the figure of a gallant Highlander. ... He had his Tartan plaid thrown about him, a large blue bonnet with a knot of black ribband like a cockade, a brown short coat of a kind of duffle, a Tartan waistcoat with gold buttons and gold button-holes, a bluish philibeg [kilt], and Tartan hose. ... There was a comfortable parlour with a good fire, and a dram of admirable Holland's gin went round. By and by supper came, when there appeared his spouse, the celebrated Miss Flora. She was a little woman, of a mild and genteel appearance, mighty soft and well-bred. To see Dr. Samuel Johnson salute Miss Flora Macdonald was a wonderful romantic scene to me. ... We had as genteel a supper as one would wish to see, in particular an excellent roasted turkey, porter to drink at table, and after supper claret and punch.' Johnson reported his stay more briefly: 'At Kingsburgh we were liberally feasted, and I slept in the bed on which the Prince reposed in his distress.' According to Boswell: 'The room where we lay was a room indeed. Each bed had tartan curtains, and Dr. Johnson's was the very bed in which the Prince lay. To see Dr. Samuel Johnson lying in Prince Charles's bed, in the Isle of Skye, in the house of Miss Flora Macdonald, struck me with such a group of ideas as it is not easy for words to describe as the mind perceives them.' Johnson encouraged Flora to recall the time she saved the Prince from capture, and said afterwards: 'All this should be written down.' This she had already ensured, by dictating her narrative to Bishop Robert Forbes at Leith.

Glasgow Punch

This was so named because of Glasgow's trade with the West Indies, the home of rum. Blending rum punch was a great skill, and many Glasgow citizens had their own special recipes. The actual punch-bowl used by Johnson and Boswell at Raasay House is now on exhibition at Eilean Donan Castle, the seat of the Macraes near Dornie in Wester Ross. The punch-bowl of the Saracen's Head Inn in Glasgow (see illustration, p. 80) was in use when Johnson and Boswell stayed there, and was probably used for the following rum punch.

6 lemons	about 2 pints water
or 4 lemons and 2 limes	(traditionally spring water)
4 oz. loaf sugar	1 bottle of rum

Rub the loaf sugar on the lemons (and the limes, if used) to extract flavour. Squeeze the juices into the punch-bowl. Gently dissolve the sugar in $\frac{1}{4}$ pint of hot water. Leave until cold. Add with the rum to the bowl; and add sufficient water for desired strength. Serve cold.

Auld Man's Milk
Adapted from Mrs. Dods's recipe.

3 eggs	$\frac{1}{4}$ pint rum, whisky or brandy
2 rounded tablespoons sugar	1 lemon, thinly peeled
1 pint single cream	grated nutmeg

Separate the eggs. Beat together the yolks and sugar, and gradually beat in the cream. Leave the spirits to infuse with the lemon peel for $\frac{1}{2}$ hour beforehand. Strain or remove the peel, and gradually add the spirits to the cream mixture. Whip the egg whites until stiff, and lightly fold in. Pour into a punch-bowl, and grate nutmeg on top. Stir, and ladle into glasses as required.

Johnson and Boswell with Allan and Flora Macdonald at Kingsburgh, attributed to Allan Ramsay
It is appropriate that a portrait of Bonnie Prince Charlie is on the wall of the home of the woman who saved his life

Gathering Dulse, by McIan
Children collecting Dulse, a chocolate-coloured marine growth which, when
washed and boiled, formed a rich gelatinous base for making soup

13th–14th September   Kingsburgh to Dunvegan, by way of Greshornish

Hosts: Norman Macleod of Macleod, and his mother Emilia Brodie, Lady Macleod

From Kingsburgh, which they left on the morning of 13th September, the travellers saved several miles by taking a boat to Greshornish, where their horses were waiting to take them on to Dunvegan Castle, the oldest inhabited seat in the continuous possession of one Highland family. 'To Dunvegan we came', wrote Johnson, 'very willing to be at rest, and found our fatigue amply recompensed by our reception. Lady Macleod, who had lived many years in England, was newly come hither with her son and four daughters, who knew all the arts of southern elegance, and all the modes of English economy.' Soon after their arrival, the young laird, Norman Macleod of Macleod, came in with his kinsman, Colonel John Macleod of Talisker, to have a meal. 'We had', said Boswell, 'venison collops from Cuillin, and something else,' followed by 'admirable tea' in the drawing-room. 'In the evening', continued Boswell, 'there was a little repast of bread and cheese and porter and wine and punch only, as we had dined so late. I had a large old bedchamber, a large old-fashioned crimson bed, a light closet with a chest of drawers. I was quite at home.' The following day the travellers surveyed the castle and its grounds, and were duly impressed. Afterwards, at dinner, their host was joined by other Macleods, including Magnus Macleod, the brother of the laird of Talisker, and they 'had admirable venison from Harris, good soup—in a word, all that a good table has'. Neither traveller mentioned the fact, but some soup in Skye was made from dulse, which according to Martin Martin 'is eat raw, and then reckon'd to be loosening, and very good for the Sight. . . . The Natives eat it boil'd with Butter, and reckon it very wholesom.'

Venison Collops

Only prime venison cuts should be used. Mrs. Dods said the dish could be improved by adding a squeeze of lemon or orange juice.

1–1¼ lb. haunch or fillet of venison	1 wine glass of claret
2 oz. (¼ cup) butter	pinch of cayenne pepper
salt and pepper	grated nutmeg
½ pint (1¼ cups) venison stock (made from the trimmings)	squeeze of lemon or orange juice
	1 tablespoon redcurrant jelly

Cut the venison into ¼ inch thick slices (or collops). Flatten with the back of a knife or a rolling-pin. Melt the butter in a frying-pan, season the collops with salt and pepper, and fry fairly quickly (3–4 minutes on each side). Remove onto an ashet, and keep warm. Add the stock and claret to the juices in the frying-pan, reduce by half. Add pinch of cayenne and nutmeg, lemon or orange juice, and redcurrant jelly, and simmer for 5 minutes. Check the seasoning. Pour the sauce over the collops, and serve hot with fried breadcrumbs or skirlie. Serves 4.

BEEF COLLOPS IN THE PAN Ingredients as above, but omit venison and redcurrant jelly and use instead fillet or rump of beef, one finely sliced onion, and beefstock. Cook the onions with the beef collops, and proceed as above.

SKIRLIE

2 oz. dripping or suet	4 oz. (1 cup) medium oatmeal
1 medium onion	salt and pepper

Melt the dripping or suet in a frying-pan. Finely chop the onion, add, and cook slowly until light brown. Sprinkle in the oatmeal, and cook slowly, stirring occasionally to prevent sticking. Continue cooking until crisp and golden brown. Season to taste. Serve hot with all game dishes, or use cold for stuffing a chicken before roasting.

Dunvegan Castle in 1772, by Griffith
Johnson and Boswell enjoyed several days here as guests of Norman Macleod of
Macleod, later a Major General

14th–21st September   At Dunvegan Castle, Isle of Skye

Hosts: Norman Macleod of Macleod, and his mother Emilia Brodie, Lady Macleod

Johnson and Boswell were guests at Dunvegan Castle for eight nights, the longest stay at one place during their whole tour, and the only way to cover that period is to give brief references to the hospitality they enjoyed. For instance, on 15th September, Boswell wrote: 'We had a venison pasty today and most excellent roast beef. But I need say no more as to dinner or supper than that there is abundance of good things genteelly served up. ... Lady Macleod, who is a heroine for the clan, entertained us like princes. She has at the same time the greatest economy. She is butler herself, even of the porter. We had porter from the cask, as in London; claret, port, sherry, and punch. ... Lady Macleod and her daughters eat oat-bread. Dr. Johnson and I had excellent cakes of flour. She is resolved to live just as the farmers do.' On

16th September Boswell reported that 'last night much care was taken of Dr. Johnson, who was still distressed by his cold. He had hitherto most strangely slept without a night-cap. Miss Macleod made him a large flannel one, and he was prevailed with to drink a little brandy when he was going to bed. He has great virtue in not drinking wine or any fermented liquor, because he could not do it in moderation.' Boswell thought 'it was wonderful how well time passed in a remote castle and in dreary weather'. Johnson was equally pleased with his stay, and the food he was given, and told a friend that 'venison came to the table every day in its various forms'. Looking back on his visit, Johnson was very complimentary. 'At Dunvegan,' he wrote, 'I had tasted lotus, and was in danger of forgetting that I was ever to depart.'

VENISON PASTY Mrs. McLintock wrote: 'Take a Haunch or Side of Venison, and bone it, take the outmost skin off, then put in the Form of a Pastry, and lay the Side you cutted the skin off downwards to the Board, and slice it cross and cross with your Knife, then season it with 2 Ounces of Salt, 1 Ounce of Pepper, a Nutmeg grated, so close up your Pasty and send it to the Oven.'
To make a Venison Pasty follow the recipe for Veal Flory (on p. 77), using stewing venison instead of veal. Omit the raisins and, if preferred, use orange instead of lemon. Cook for 2 hours, and add a glass of claret before serving. Serve with rowan jelly (see p. 65).

Braised Haunch of Venison

2–2½ lb. haunch of venison	½ pint (1¼ cups) stock
2 oz. dripping	salt
2 oz. (½ cup) flour	2 tablespoons redcurrant jelly

for the marinade

⅛ pint (⅓ cup) olive oil	¼ head celery, sliced
⅛ pint (⅓ cup) vinegar	pinch of thyme
½ pint (1¼ cups) red wine	2 bay leaves
1 onion, sliced	12 peppercorns
1 carrot, sliced	6 juniper berries

Mix together all the marinade ingredients in an earthenware bowl, add the venison, and leave to marinade for two days, turning occasionally. Remove the venison, and wipe dry. Melt the dripping in a heavy pan, place in the venison, and seal the outside. Remove the venison, and place in a large ovenware dish with a lid. Add the flour to the dripping, and cook to form a brown roux. Gradually stir in the stock, marinade (with vegetables), and bring to the boil. Add a little salt. Pour over the haunch, cover, and place in a pre-heated very moderate oven, Gas No. 3 : 325°F., for 2–2½ hours, or until cooked. Remove the haunch, and place on a serving dish. Strain the sauce into a saucepan and reduce to a coating consistency. Stir in the redcurrant jelly, and check the seasoning. Coat the venison with a little of the sauce, and serve the remainder separately. Serves 6–8.

Angling, by McIan
Johnson and Boswell watched children angling when they were at Ullinish

21st–23rd September　Dunvegan to Ullinish, by way of Duirinish

Host: Alexander Macleod of Ullinish, Sheriff-Substitute of Skye

On 21st September, the travellers left Dunvegan Castle and, after a stop at Duirinish to look at the parish churchyard, they made their way to Ullinish Lodge, the home of Alexander Macleod of Ullinish, the only official representative of the law on Skye. They arrived at 'about six o'clock, and found a very good farmhouse, of two storeys'. Their host was 'a plain honest man in brown, much like an English Justice'. His daughter Mary was 'a very well-bred girl' who had never been out of Skye. 'Though we came so late,' wrote Boswell, 'we had dinner, tea, and supper. I had a good room at night.' The next day, 22nd September, the travellers walked to see what they believed were the remains of the thirteenth-century stronghold of Leod of the Isle of Man, ancestor of all the Macleods. On returning to Ullinish they were told of a cave, 'remarkable for the powerful reverberation of sounds', and after dinner they took a boat to see this 'curious cavity'. 'Here', said Johnson, 'I saw what I had never seen before, limpets and mussels in their natural state.' 'We found', he continued, 'a little boy upon the point of a rock, catching with his angle, a supper for the family. We rowed up to him, and borrowed his rod, with which Mr. Boswell caught a cuddy. . . . It is not much bigger than a gudgeon, but is of great use in these Islands, as it affords the lower people both food, and oil for their lamps. They are caught like whitebait in the Thames.' Boswell's version is slightly different, as to number and sex of the children. He wrote: 'Dr. Johnson had never catched any fish in the sea. Two little girls were fishing from a rock. We borrowed their lines, and Dr. Johnson drew one or two cuddies, but he let them go again.'

Although the travellers never recorded what they had to eat at Ullinish, their interest in angling suggested the recipes chosen for this page.

Potted Herrings

'To pot fresh herrings,' wrote Mrs. Frazer, 'scale them, and make them very clean; season them well with salt and spices, pack them neatly in your potting can, laying the shoulders of one to the tail of the other. . . . Pour on as much vinegar as will cover them; bind them close up, and put them in a slow oven. They will take about four hours of doing.'

8 herrings	1 tablespoon pickling spice
salt and pepper	4 bay leaves
$\frac{3}{4}$ pint (2 cups) malt vinegar and water, mixed	2 small onions, cut into rings

Scale, clean, split, and bone the herrings. Sprinkle well with salt and pepper, and roll up the fillets from head to tail. Mix together the vinegar and water and pickling spice. Place the bay leaves and half the onion rings in the base of an ovenware dish. Pack in the rolled fillets. Pour the vinegar mixture over them, and sprinkle on the remainder of the onion rings. Cover tightly with foil or a lid, and bake very slowly, Gas No. 1: 290°F., for $1\frac{1}{2}$ hours. Leave covered until cool. Mackerel and trout can be prepared in the same way.

HERRINGS IN OATMEAL　Mrs. Dods wrote: 'In Scotland herrings are often dipped in oatmeal, and fried in plenty of dripping with sliced onion.' Today it is more common to omit the onion. Trout can be treated in the same way.

HERRING PIE　Mrs. McLintock said: 'Cut the Heads, Fins and Tails off them; season them with Salt and Pepper, lay them in your Pye with a good store of Butter and Onions, so close it and send it to the Oven.'

Grinding the Quern and Waulking the Cloth, by Griffith
Women at Talisker shrinking or waulking a finished web of cloth, which they did
to the rhythm of special Gaelic 'waulking songs'. On the left two women grind
meal in a quern.

23rd–25th September   Ullinish to Talisker, by way of Ferinlea

Hosts: Colonel John Macleod of Talisker, and his wife Mary Maclean of Coll

After two restful nights at Ullinish, Johnson and Boswell set out by boat to Talisker, where the best whisky in Skye is made. They actually landed at Ferinlea, where they found Alexander Macleod of Ferinlea waiting on the shore to greet them. His wife Margaret was one of the twenty-five children of the celebrated Donald Macleod of Bernera, known as 'The Old Trojan', because of his virility and martial skills. Recording his visit to Ferinlea, Boswell wrote: 'We had here an excellent dinner, in particular a remarkable leg of boiled mutton with turnips and carrots.' After this meal the travellers rode three miles to Talisker to stay with the laird. 'At Talisker,' said Boswell, 'we found Mrs. Macleod, the Colonel's lady, a civil genteel woman. ... We found here too Donald Maclean, the young Laird of Coll (nephew to Talisker). I had a letter to him from his uncle, Professor Macleod at Aberdeen. Dr. Johnson said he was a fine fellow. ... Our tea was in good order, and we had a genteel supper. The Colonel had claret, port, sherry, and punch, with porter in abundance.' Johnson, in a letter to a friend, wrote: 'We passed two days at Talisker very happily, both by the pleasantness of the place and elegance of our reception. ... Talisker has long been in the possession of a gentleman, and, therefore, has a garden well cultivated. ... Their punch is made without lemons or any substitute.' They left Talisker at noon on 25th September. 'We stopped', wrote Boswell, 'at a little hut, where we saw an old woman grinding with the quern.' Johnson noted the same practice: 'The housewives grind their oats with a quern, or handmill, which consists of two stones.' He had also been shown 'the operation of *wawking* cloth, that is, thickening it as done by a mill. ... It is performed by women, who kneel upon the ground, and rub it with both their hands, singing an Erse (Gaelic) song all the time.'

Boiled Gigot of Mutton

1 gigot (leg) of mutton, approx. 5 lb.	salt and pepper
¾ lb. small onions	faggot of herbs
¾ lb. small carrots	¾ lb. turnips

Ask the butcher to remove the pelvic bone (to make carving easier). Trim off the excess fat. Weigh the meat, and allow 25 minutes to each lb., and 25 minutes over. Rub the meat with salt and pepper, place in a large saucepan, cover with cold water, bring to the boil, remove the scum, and add about 2 teaspoons salt. Slice one onion and one carrot, and add with faggot of herbs. Cover, and allow to simmer gently until about 1 hour before the end of the cooking time. Add the turnip (cut into neat pieces) and the remainder of the onions and carrots, and continue simmering until cooked. Do not boil, or the meat will become stringy. Remove the meat, whole carrots, onions, and turnip, and keep warm. Reduce the stock rapidly for the caper sauce. Strain, and measure off 1 pint for the sauce.

CAPER SAUCE Adapted from Mrs. Frazer's suggestion as an accompaniment to boiled gigot of mutton.

1½ oz. butter	1 pint (2½ cups) stock
1½ oz. flour	1 oz. capers

Melt the butter, stir in the flour, and cook gently for 1–2 minutes. Gradually stir in the hot stock, bring to the boil, and simmer for 5 minutes. Stir in the capers, a little of the caper vinegar, and check the seasoning. Carve the meat, and place on a hot ashet. Garnish with the carrots, onions, and turnip, and pour a little of the hot stock over the dish. Serve the caper sauce separately. Serves 6–8. For a small family use only the shank-end piece of the gigot.

25th–27th September   Talisker to Coirechatachan (or Corrie), by way of Sconser

Hosts: Lachlan Mackinnon of Corrie, and his third wife Anne Macdonald of Kingsburgh

Accompanied by young Donald Maclean of Coll (always known as 'Young Coll'), the travellers rode from Talisker by way of Sligachan to the inn belonging to James Macdonald at Sconser, which was in 'a poor state'; and then, sending on their horses by road, they took a boat to Strollamus, two miles from the home of Mackinnon of Corrie. Here, for the first time during the tour, they paid a second visit to one of their hosts. 'We were', wrote Boswell, 'most hospitably received by the master and mistress, who were just going to bed, but, with unaffected ready kindness, made a good fire, and at twelve o'clock at night had supper on the table.' Johnson went to bed as soon as he had eaten, but Boswell stayed up drinking punch with his host and Young Coll until five in the morning. 'I awakened at noon,' continued Boswell,

'with a severe headache', and it took some of Mackinnon's brandy to help in his recovery from heavy drinking. For three nights the travellers stayed with the generous Mackinnons who, in common with most of the people of Skye, had much impressed Johnson. 'At the tables where a stranger is received,' he said, 'neither plenty nor delicacy is wanting. ... The moorgame is everywhere to be had [and] the sea abounds with fish. ... The Isle of Skye has stags and roebucks, but no hares. They sell very numerous droves of oxen yearly to England, and therefore cannot be supposed to want beef at home. Sheep and goats are in great numbers, and they have the common domestic fowls. ... Geese seem to be of a middle race, between the wild and domestic kinds.'

Bread and Butter Pudding

Enjoyed by the travellers on their first visit to Corrie (see p. 35).

marinade for 1 hour:
2 oz. ($\frac{1}{2}$ cup) raisins
1 oz. ($\frac{1}{4}$ cup) citron peel
juice of $\frac{1}{2}$ orange
2 tablespoons brandy or rum

4 slices white bread, liberally buttered
1 pint ($2\frac{1}{2}$ cups) milk
3 eggs
2 oz. ($\frac{1}{4}$ cup) sugar
nutmeg

Leave the fruit to marinade for 1 hour. Cut each slice of bread diagonally into four. Butter the inside of a medium-sized pie-dish. Heat the milk, and pour onto the beaten eggs and sugar to make the custard. Place a layer of bread in the dish. Sprinkle on the marinaded fruit, and finally arrange the remaining bread on top. Pour on half the custard, and leave to stand for 10 minutes. Pour on the remaining custard, and grate nutmeg on top. Place the pie-dish in a roasting-tin, half-filled with hot water, and place in the middle of a very moderate oven, Gas No. 3: 325°F., for about 1 hour, until the custard is set, and the top is a pale golden brown. (The tin of water prevents the custard from overcooking, and separating.) Serve hot with cream. Serves 4.

Velvet Cream (or Curds and Cream)
Adapted from Mrs. Maciver's recipe.

1 pint ($2\frac{1}{2}$ cups) milk
1 teaspoon rennet
1 level tablespoon sugar

nutmeg
$\frac{1}{4}$ pint ($\frac{2}{3}$ cup) double cream

Heat the milk in a saucepan to blood-heat only. Stir in the rennet and sugar, and pour immediately into a glass bowl. Leave without moving until it sets as velvet cream. Grate nutmeg on top liberally. Whip the cream, sweeten with a little sugar, and serve with the velvet cream. This dish can be flavoured with a few drops of rum, brandy, or vanilla. For lemon or orange flavour, thinly peel the rind from the fruit, and leave to infuse in the lukewarm milk for 15 minutes. Strain, and use as before.

The Recovery, by Rowlandson
Dr. Johnson smugly watches Boswell trying to recover from a bout of heavy drinking at Corrie. Above Boswell's head is a picture of a pig, the symbol of self-indulgence.

Carrying home the Peat, by McIan
Women using the traditional creels for carrying loads of peat

28th September–3rd October Corrie to Armadale, staying *en route* at Ostaig

Hosts: Rev. Martin Macpherson, Minister of Sleat, and his wife Mary Mackinnon of Corrie at Ostaig Manse; and James Macdonald of Tormore, factor and baron-bailie to Sir Alexander Macdonald of Sleat, Bt., at Armadale

On 28th September the travellers left the Mackinnons of Corrie. 'Our kind host and hostess', wrote Boswell, 'would not let us go without taking a *snatch*, as they called it, which was in truth a very good dinner.' That evening, accompanied by Young Coll, they arrived at Ostaig Manse to stay with Mackinnon's daughter Mary, and her husband Rev. Martin Macpherson. They were received 'with much kindness', and the minister's sister Isabella 'pleased Dr. Johnson much, by singing Erse songs, and playing on the guitar'. On 1st October, after two nights at Ostaig, the travellers and Young Coll moved on to Armadale to stay with James Macdonald, baron-bailie to Sir Alexander Macdonald, who had now left the island to live in Edinburgh. On 2nd October Boswell noted that they had 'a good dinner, and in the evening a great dance'. Although not fond of dancing he said: 'We made out five country squares without sitting down' and also admitted: 'I danced a reel tonight to the music of the bagpipe, which I never did before.' Johnson, who did not dance at all, was more interested in making general observations about Skye. He wrote: 'I gathered gooseberries, but they were small, and the husk was thick. . . . The goats and sheep are milked like the cows. . . . Sheep's milk is never eaten before it is boiled. As it is thick, it must be very liberal or curd,' and it was often made into small cheeses. 'The only fuel of the Islands is peat. . . . It appears to be a mass of black earth held together by vegetable fibres. . . . They cut it into square pieces, and pile it up to dry beside the house. . . . It burns well in grates, and in the best houses is so used.'

The 'snatch' (or the snack) given to the travellers was more substantial than its modern counterpart. Highland gamekeepers and gillies still use the term 'Snatch' for the large cold meal most of them carry when they are out on the moors all day. Food chosen for a modern 'snack' would include cakes or teabread.

Cherry and Nut Teabread

6 oz. (1½ cups) plain flour
1½ level teaspoons baking-powder
½ level teaspoon mixed spice
3 oz. (⅜ cup) margarine

2 oz. (½ cup) hazel nuts, chopped
2 oz. (½ cup) glacé cherries, chopped
4 oz. (1 cup) demerara sugar
7 tablespoons of milk

Sieve the flour, baking-powder and spice into a mixing bowl. Add the fat, and rub in with fingertips. Stir in the chopped nuts, cherries, and 3 oz. of the demerara sugar. Finally, add the milk, and mix with a knife to a fairly stiff dough. Place the mixture in a well greased 1 lb. bread-tin, sprinkle the top with the remaining sugar. Bake in the middle of a pre-heated moderate oven, Gas No. 4: 350°F., for 1–1¼ hours. Remove, and cool on a wire rack. If preferred, the cherries can be omitted, and 2 oz. chopped crystalized ginger added with 1 level teaspoon of ground ginger instead of mixed spice.

Seed Cake

Adapted from Mrs. Cleland's recipe.

8 oz. (2 cups) plain flour
1½ level teaspoons baking-powder
6 oz. (¾ cup) butter or margarine
6 oz. (¾ cup) caster (fine) sugar

3 eggs
1 tablespoon caraway seeds
2 tablespoons brandy

Sieve together the flour and baking-powder. Place the butter in a bowl, and beat until soft. Add the sugar, and continue beating until the mixture is light and creamy. Gradually beat in the eggs. Add a spoonful of the flour to prevent the mixture curdling. Beat in the caraway seeds. Using a metal spoon, gradually fold in the sieved flour and, finally, the brandy (if used). Place in a 7-inch cake-tin, previously lined with greased paper. Bake in the middle of a pre-heated very moderate oven, Gas No. 3: 325°F., for approx. 1½ hours. Cool for a few minutes, and turn out onto a wire rack.

3rd–4th October   Sailing from the Isle of Skye to the Isle of Coll

Host: Captain John Simson, from Islay, master of a twelve-ton trading sloop

On the morning of 3rd October, Johnson and Boswell and Young Coll set sail from Armadale in a ship belonging to John Simson, who had also been staying with Bailie James Macdonald, and had been waiting for a fair wind to take him to the Isle of Mull. After a few hours at sea, it began to rain. Dr. Johnson became sick, and retired under cover. 'I kept above,' said Boswell, 'that I might have fresh air. I eat bread and cheese, and drank whisky and rum and brandy. The worthy Bailie had sent with us half a sheep and biscuits and apples and beer and brandy. There was a little room or den at the forecastle, with two beds, and a fire in it. Dinner was dressed, and I was persuaded to go down. I eat boiled mutton and boiled salt herring, and drank beer and punch. I exulted in being a stout seaman, while Dr. Johnson was quite in a state of annihilation.' Passing the point of Ardnamurchan the wind changed. 'As we advanced,' continued Boswell, 'the storm grew greater, and the sea very rough.' Instead of making for Mull, it was decided it was safer to run before the wind and make for Coll, especially as it was getting dark. Young Coll took over command of the ship, as he knew those waters well. The storm grew worse, and the sails 'were in danger of being torn to pieces'. Boswell noted: 'Our vessel often lay so much on one side, that I trembled lest she should be overset.' Young Coll remained calm and by fine seamanship brought the vessel safely to anchor in a harbour at Coll in the middle of the night. Throughout the storm Dr. Johnson had remained under cover, with one of Coll's greyhounds at his back to keep him warm. On the morning of 4th October, the travellers went ashore on an island they had never intended to visit. Boswell, much subdued by his experience in the storm, was no longer convinced that he was a stout seaman.

Tatties an' Herrin'

Mrs. Dods wrote: 'Take two or three pickled herrings, put them in a stone jar, fill it up with potatoes, and a little water, and let it bake in the oven until done.' They were traditionally cooked in a three-legged pot over a fire.

4 fresh or salted herrings	salt and pepper
1½ lb. new or mealy potatoes	butter

Soak the herrings (if salted) overnight. Scrub the new (preferably even-sized) potatoes, or peel old potatoes and cut into equal-sized pieces. Half cover with water (and add salt, if fresh herrings are used). Cook for about 15 minutes. Lay the prepared fish on top of the potatoes, cover tightly, and cook for a further 15 minutes. Lift out the fish carefully onto a hot ashet. Drain, and return the potatoes to the stove to dry, place them around the fish, and serve with plenty of butter and oatcakes (see p. 19). Serves 4.

Potted Hough

1 nap bone (veal knuckle)	salt and pepper
2 lb. hough (shin of beef)	faggot of herbs

Ask the butcher to saw the nap bone. Slice the hough. Place in a pan, just cover with cold water, bring to the boil, remove scum, add about 2 teaspoons salt, pepper, and faggot of herbs. Leave to simmer very slowly for 5–6 hours, or place in an earthenware dish and leave in a very low oven overnight. Strain the stock into a clean pan, removing the herbs, and allow to reduce. Place the meat on a board, discard the bone and gristle, and shred the meat. Add the shredded meat to the reducing stock, check the seasoning, boil for a few minutes, remove from the heat, and allow to cool, stirring occasionally. Pour into one large wetted mould, or into 8 individual moulds, and leave until set. If, before pouring into the moulds, the stock does not appear to be jellying, add one teaspoon of gelatine dissolved in a little water.

Sailing among the Hebrides, by Rowlandson
As the fury of the storm increases, Boswell's bonnet flies off in the wind. His companion, young Donald Maclean of Coll, advises him to hold on to the rope.

55

4th–5th October　On the Isle of Coll, at Achamore and Grishipoll

Hosts: Captain Lachlan Maclean of Achamore, and his wife Florence Maclean; Rev. Hector Maclean,
Minister of Coll and Tiree, and his wife Janet Maclean; and Sween Macsween, of the White House at Grishipoll

As soon as the travellers went ashore on 4th October, Young Coll took them directly to nearby Achamore, the home of Captain Lachlan Maclean, who had served for many years in the army of the East India Company. 'There was a blazing peat-fire,' wrote Boswell, 'and Mrs. Maclean, the daughter of the minister of the parish, got us tea. ... The day slipped along easily enough. We had a very good dinner: the best shortbread just baked by Mrs. Maclean, and pleasant rum punch soured with lemon shrub.' After a night at Achamore, the travellers visited Captain Lachlan Maclean's father-in-law (and uncle) Rev. Hector Maclean, who lived in the centre of Coll in a farm-house which served as his manse. The minister was 'a decent old man in a full suit of black and a black wig,' which made Johnson think that he was 'as well dressed and had as much dignity as the dean of a cathedral'. They met his wife and his younger daughter, Margaret, who served them with 'a glass of whisky and cheese and barley-bread'. Johnson and the minister, both slightly deaf, had a forceful debate on religion, during which neither heard the subtle points the other was making. This caused misunderstanding, and some annoyance to both men, but Johnson liked the minister and was pleased he was 'so orthodox'. From the 'manse' the travellers rode to Grishipoll, stopping *en route* to view the old burial ground of the Macleans of Coll. The White House of Grishipoll was held by Young Coll's tenant and foster-father, a Skyeman called Sween Macsween. It was 'an excellent slated house of two storeys' where, said Johnson, 'I saw more of the ancient life of a Highlander, than I had yet found. Mrs. Macsween could speak no English ... but she was hospitable and good-humoured. ... We found tea here, as in every other place, but our spoons were of horn.' Boswell said: 'We had here the best goose that I ever eat. Dr. Johnson was much pleased with it', and added: 'Whisky was served round in a shell, according to the ancient Highland custom.' Johnson had no whisky, but 'drank some water out of the shell'. The travellers stayed the night at Grishipoll.

Shortbread

Recipes for shortbread abound in old Scottish cookery-books. The one given here includes a little rice flour, which improves the texture.

10 oz. plain flour ⎫ *or* 12 oz. (3 cups)		8 oz. (1 cup) butter
2 oz. rice flour ⎬ of plain flour		4 oz. (½ cup) caster
		(fine) sugar

Sieve the flour onto a board. Add the butter and sugar, and knead together with the hand until a smooth dough is formed. Divide into two, and flatten into rounds, ½–¾ inch in thickness. Pinch up the edges, and place carefully on a baking-tray lined with grease-proof paper. Prick all over with a fork. Mark each round into 8 with a knife. Dust with caster sugar, and bake in the middle of a very moderate oven, Gas No. 2: 300°F., for 40–50 minutes. The shortbread should be pale in colour when baked. If preferred, roll the shortbread to a strip 3 inches wide by ½ inch thick, and cut into 1-inch fingers. Bake for 20 minutes.

PITCAITHLY BANNOCK　As for shortbread, with the addition of 2 oz. chopped citron peel and 2 oz. chopped almonds. Decorate the top with peel, and bake as before.

Johnson and Boswell with Rev. Hector Maclean, by Kay
Boswell sits quietly while Johnson disputes some points of theology with the
Minister of Coll

57

The Island of Coll, with Fishermen and Boats, by Poole
Breacacha Castle, the old stronghold of the Macleans of Coll, with Breacacha
House in the background. Both buildings appear as Johnson and Boswell saw them.

5th–11th October   At Breacacha House, Isle of Coll

Host: Donald Maclean, Younger of Coll ('Young Coll'), eldest son of the absent laird, Hugh Maclean of Coll

After dinner at Grishipoll on 5th October the travellers were guided by their host's son, Hugh Macsween, to Breacacha House, the seat of the Maclean chieftains of Coll. Here, they were entertained until 11th October by their friend Young Coll, whose father was absent in Aberdeen with the rest of his family. The 'very good supper served on china,' which they had as soon as they arrived, was accompanied by 'a bold tune from the piper, a decent comely fellow with a green cloth waistcoat with silver lace. ... His name was Neil Rankin,' and, as Boswell correctly noted, 'these Rankins have been pipers to the family of Maclean for many generations'. Breacacha House was a 'neat new-built gentleman's house' of three storeys, with four rooms on each floor, and two wings or pavilions. Boswell thought that it was the best place he had visited since leaving Slains Castle, but Johnson remarked 'that there was nothing becoming a chief about it. It was quite a tradesman's box.' The next morning the travellers carefully surveyed the former home of the Coll chieftains, Breacacha Castle, which was only 'two gun-shots from the present house, very near the shore'. It had last been lived in by Young Coll's uncle, who had died in 1754. During their stay with Young Coll the travellers met several of his tenants, including Neil Maclean, who was the holder of the small farm at Crossapoll at the south end of the island. Johnson found the whole island fascinating. 'Coll', he wrote, 'has many lochs, some of which have trout and eels. ... In every house candles are made, both moulded and dipped. Their wicks are small shreds of linen cloth. They all know how to extract from the cuddy oil for their lamps. They all tan skins and make brogues. ... Whisky is very plentiful: there are several stills in the island.' Boswell added: 'There are snipe, wild-duck, wild-geese, and swans, in winter; wild pidgeons, plover, and great numbers of starlings; of which I shot some, and found them pretty good eating.' He also said: 'We really lived plentifully here. ... We had wheat bread, both loaf and biscuit. ... There was abundance of cream both at dinner and supper.'

Quick Wheaten Bread

8 oz. (2 cups) brown flour	½ pint (1¼ cups) lukewarm
8 oz. (2 cups) plain white flour	water
1 level teaspoon of salt	1 oz. melted fat or oil
2 level teaspoons of sugar	½ oz. fresh yeast

Place the two flours, salt, and sugar in a warm bowl. Dissolve the yeast in the lukewarm water with the melted fat or oil. Pour into the bowl, and mix to a fairly stiff dough. If too soft, add a little more flour. Turn onto a lightly-floured board and knead for 2–3 minutes, until smooth. Have ready, two 1 lb. greased bread-tins. Divide the dough into two. Shape each of the pieces, and fit into the tins. Press down with the knuckles. Brush the tops with ½ teaspoon of salt dissolved in one tablespoon of hot water, and leave covered in a warm place to rise to the tops of the tins. Bake near the top of a pre-heated hot oven, Gas No. 7: 425°F., for 30–40 minutes. Turn out and, if the bread is cooked, the base will sound hollow when tapped. Cool on a wire rack.

Roast Larks

These are cooked in the same manner as roast starling. 'To roast larks,' wrote Mrs. Cleland, 'put them on a Skewer, tye them to the Spit, baste them and drudge them with Crumbs of Bread and Salt; then have Crumbs of Bread and lay it in the dish with them.'

The White House of Grishipoll, by Lauchlan Maclean
Drawn in 1852, this is the earliest known picture of the White House. The cow, although charming, has more than a passing resemblance to a friendly lioness.

11th–14th October   On the Isle of Coll, at Achamore and Grishipoll

Hosts: Captain Lachlan Maclean of Achamore, and his wife Florence Maclean; Sween Macsween, of the White House at Grishipoll; and Captain Hugh Macdonald, master of a kelp trading sloop, lying off Coll

On 11th October the travellers went down to the harbour to set sail for Mull, but a violent storm occurred, and they were obliged to take shelter at Achamore with Captain Lachlan Maclean, with whom they dined and spent the night. The following day another storm again prevented them from leaving the island, and they went to stay the night with Sween Macsween at the White House at Grishipoll, 'where', said Boswell, 'we arrived very wet, fatigued, and hungry. . . . We had at last a good dinner, or rather supper, and were very well satisfied with our entertainment.' Johnson remarked to Boswell: 'You must consider, sir, a dinner here is a matter of great consequence. It is a thing to be first planned and then executed. I suppose the mutton was brought some miles off, from some place where they knew there was a sheep killed.' Boswell noted: 'There is here the bird called a curlew. It is a sucking bird, like a woodcock, but as large as a wild duck. We had two to dinner one day. They eat pretty well, and had no fishy taste. . . . Solan geese fly about Coll, but do not breed here.' Boswell also noted the skills of the people of Coll, and found they could all dye cloth. 'Heath is used for yellow; and for red, a moss which grows on stones. They make broad-cloth, and tartan, and linen, of their own wool and flax. . . . Hard-ware and several small articles are brought annually from Greenock and are sold in the only shop in the island.' On 13th October, the travellers tried for the third time to set sail, but once more the wind was against them. Having boarded the sloop, a kelp trader belonging to Hugh Macdonald, they 'resolved not to go ashore again' and spent the day reading in the cabin, where they had a meal of mutton and potatoes. That night they slept on board and, finally, on the following morning the anchor was hauled, and they left for Mull, with Young Coll as their companion.

Roast Goose and Grosset Sauce

Enjoyed by the travellers on their first visit to Grishipoll (see p. 57). Mrs. Cleland, writing about goose, said: 'Stuff it with boiled Potatoes, and Onions, chopped small, seasoned with Pepper and Salt; or you may stuff it with Apples.' Mrs. Maciver suggested serving gooseberry or grosset sauce with goose; and this sauce can also be served with duck, roast pork, and grilled mackerel. In the eighteenth century sorrel juice was added to the goose-berries.

1 goose, 8–9 lb.	2 tablespoons of lard

for potato and onion stuffing:
1 lb. cooked mashed potatoes
2 finely chopped onions
1 teaspoon chopped sage
salt and pepper

for grosset sauce:
1 lb. gooseberries
1 tablespoon sugar
1 tablespoon butter
2 tablespoons water

Prepare the goose, and cook the giblets with an onion to make stock for the gravy. Mix together all the stuffing ingredients, season well, stuff the goose and secure with a skewer or string. Season the goose on the outside with salt and pepper, place in a roasting-tin, spread the lard on the breast and roast in a fairly hot oven, Gas No. 5: 375°F., allowing 20 minutes for each lb. and 20 minutes over. Baste during cooking time. If preferred, the goose can be covered with foil during cooking. When cooked, remove the goose, and the skewer or string, and leave to stand in a warm place for 10–15 minutes. This allows the juices to settle, and makes carving much easier. Drain off the fat, leaving the sediment in the pan. Add ¾ pint giblet stock, and allow to simmer. Season with salt and pepper. Pour into a sauce-boat. Serves 6–8.

GROSSET SAUCE   Top and tail the gooseberries, and stew with the sugar, butter, and water until soft. Rub through a sieve, or make into a purée in a liquidizer. Serve hot with the goose.

Tobermory on the Isle of Mull, by Daniell
At the bottom of the harbour lies the Spanish galleon *Florencia*, a treasure ship of
the Armada, sunk by the Macleans in 1588. Its fortune in gold, owned by the
Duke of Argyll, has never been recovered.

14th–16th October   Isle of Coll to Tobermory, Isle of Mull

Host: Catherine Maclean of Coll, wife of Dr. Hector Maclean of Gruline, at Erray House

'After a pleasant voyage, we got safely and agreeably into the harbour of Tobermory', wrote Boswell about the sea journey on 14th October. At Macarthur's Inn in Tobermory, Johnson put himself into a good humour with 'a dish of tea, some good wheaten cakes (scones) and fresh butter'. Later, while Young Coll went off to arrange accommodation for them all with his aunt Mrs. Catherine Maclean at Erray House, a mile north of Tobermory, Johnson and Boswell stayed in Macarthur's Inn and had a dinner of 'tongue and fowls and greens'. On their arrival at Erray House, the travellers 'were received by Mrs. Maclean, a little brisk old woman in a bedgown with a brown wig, and Miss (Christina) Maclean, a little plump elderly young lady' who wore 'a smart beaver hat with a white feather'. Dr. Hector Maclean was away from home. Although they had eaten a big dinner at the inn, the travellers were given a large meal. 'We had', said Boswell, 'beef collops, potatoes, sowans and cream for supper. Dr. Johnson took sowans and cream heartily. We had a bowl of rum punch.' For breakfast the next morning they were given 'currant jelly', and for dinner the same day, 'roasted turkey'. During the day they diverted themselves by looking through their host's library. Boswell studied Dr. Maclean's 'manuscript history of the Macleans' and Miss Maclean helped to entertain Johnson by translating into English some Gaelic poems, and by playing 'several tunes on a spinet'. Dr. Johnson was much impressed by Miss Maclean, and told Boswell: 'She is the most accomplished lady that I have found in the Highlands. She knows French, music, and drawing, sews neatly, makes shell-work, and can milk cows; in short, she can do everything.' On the road, after leaving Erray House on 16th October, the travellers met Dr. Hector Maclean on his way home.

Minced Beef Collops

1 lb. shoulder or topside steak, minced
1 rounded tablespoon suet or dripping
1 medium onion, finely chopped
salt and pepper
1 tablespoon mushroom ketchup
approx. $\frac{1}{2}$ pint ($1\frac{1}{4}$ cups) stock
1 heaped tablespoon oatmeal, toasted
2 slices of toast

Melt the fat in a thick-bottomed pan, add the onion and cook until golden brown. Add the meat and brown carefully, making sure the grains of meat are kept separate with a wooden spoon. Stir in the seasoning, mushroom ketchup and just enough stock to moisten. Stir again to separate the grains of meat, and simmer for 30 minutes, stirring occasionally. Add the oatmeal and simmer for 10 minutes. Check the seasoning, and serve very hot with sippets (or triangles) of toast. Serves 4. Minced hare or venison can be prepared in the same way, using $\frac{1}{2}$ stock and $\frac{1}{2}$ red wine.

SOWANS John Caird wrote: 'This dish is very generally made throughout Scotland, forms a very light supper, and is very often used in feverish cases where light diet is required. Take the inner sheelings of oats when making oatmeal, mix them with a small quantity of the meal, then lay them in water in a stone trough, or other large vessel, according to the quantity wanted. After steeping two or three days they turn sour, they are then stirred, and the seeds wrung out (the seeds are then washed in more water, which serves to asteep the next parcel). The liquor, which is wrung out, is set past for twelve hours, it grows clear, and as much of it is poured off as leaves the remains, when stirred, a sufficient thickness. But, if when tasted, it should prove too sour, pour on more water and stir well. After it clears, pour off the water as before, and repeat this until you have them to your taste. When ready put the liquor through a hair sieve, put them into a metal pot on the fire, and keep stirring until they are well boiled. They grow thick as hasty pudding. Add salt before you take them off the fire, pour them in dishes, and serve with half milk, half cream, in a bason by itself. Some chuse ale or beer.'

View of Ben More from Ulva House, by Daniell
The small isle of Ulva has been immortalized in Thomas Campbell's poem
Lord Ullin's Daughter. Ben More is the highest mountain in Mull.

16th–17th October Tobermory, Isle of Mull, to the Isle of Ulva

Hosts: Lachlan Macquarrie of Ulva, and his second wife Ann Macquarrie of Ormaig

From Tobermory the travellers, still accompanied by Young Coll, made slow progress across the north of Mull, as they were mounted on small shelties, some without halters and bridles. Johnson was made irritable by this uncomfortable ride, and by the loss of his famous oak-stick, which he had owned since 1766. By nightfall they reached a point opposite the small isle of Ulva, the home of Lachlan Macquarrie. By luck, an Ulster ship was lying in the Sound of Ulva, and its captain obligingly ferried the travellers over to the island. Boswell wrote: 'Macquarrie's house was mean; but we were agreeably surprised with the appearance of the master, whom we found to be intelligent, polite, and much a man of the world. ... He told us, his family had possessed Ulva for nine hundred years; but I was distressed to hear that it was soon to be sold for the payment of his debts.' Lachlan Macquarrie's first wife had been Alicia, a sister of Lachlan Maclean, the laird of Torloisk in Mull, who, in 1786, was visited by Bartholomé Faujas de St. Fond. Among the food mentioned by the Frenchman was porridge, which he called 'a sort of pap; oatmeal and water. In eating this thick pap, each spoonful is plunged alternately into cream, which is always alongside.' He also mentioned the preserves which were eaten with native unleavened bread, especially 'currant jelly' and 'conserve of myrtle', although bramble, rowan, and rizer jellies, and marmalade, were also much enjoyed. Johnson commented on the native bread. 'In most houses', he wrote, 'there is wheat flour, with which we were sure to be treated, if we stayed long enough to have it kneaded and baked. As neither yeast nor leaven are used among them, their bread of every kind is unfermented. They make only cakes, and never mould a loaf.'

Bramble Jelly

3 lb. brambles (blackberries)	water
1 lb. cooking apples	sugar

Remove stalks and leaves and wash the brambles. Place in a preserving-pan with roughly chopped apples (no need to peel them). Barely cover with water, and simmer slowly until soft and mushy, about 30 minutes. Scald a clean cloth or jelly-bag, and allow the mixture to drip through (but do not rub or press). Measure the juice, and allow 1 lb. sugar to each pint of juice. Return to a clean preserving-pan, stir to dissolve the sugar, bring to the boil, and fast boil for approx. 15 minutes (or to 220°F. on a sugar thermometer) until the jelly reaches setting point. If correct, the jelly will wrinkle on top when a little is placed on a *cold* saucer. Remove any scum, and pour into warm jars. Cover, and label. Makes approx. 4 lb. jelly.

ROWAN (or RODDEN) JELLY As for bramble jelly, but using 3 lb. rowan berries, and 2 lb. cooking or crab apples. Allow to simmer for about 45 minutes before dripping through a jelly-bag.

Use small jars, and serve with game or mutton dishes.

RIZER (or REDCURRANT) JELLY As for bramble jelly, omitting apples, and using 3 lb. redcurrants. Black and white currants can also be used.

Marmalade

Adapted from Mrs. McLintock's recipe for 'Marmalet of Oranges & Lemons'.

1½ lb. Seville oranges	2½ pints water
2 lemons	3 lb. sugar

Scrub the fruit well, and place in a pan. Add the water, cover, and simmer slowly for 2 hours, until the fruit is soft. Remove onto a board, cool, and cut up into chunks. Keep the pips, add to the fruit juice, and reboil for 10–15 minutes. Pass through a strainer into a preserving-pan. Add the fruit and sugar to the juice, stir until the sugar is dissolved, and fast boil until setting point is reached (see bramble jelly). Pot, cover, and label. For those who like dark marmalade, add 1 tablespoon of black treacle with the sugar.

Remains of the Chapel on Inchkenneth, by Daniell
The island (or *inch*) was probably named after Abbot Kenneth Mackenzie of
Iona, who died in 1489. His fine effigy is in the Abbey of Iona.

17th–19th October Isle of Ulva to Inchkenneth

Host: Lt.-Colonel Sir Allan Maclean of Duart & Brolas, 6th Bt. of Morvern

On the morning of 17th October the travellers, with Young Coll, were ferried from Ulva to the very small island called Inchkenneth, which was leased by Sir Allan Maclean, who, with two of his three daughters and his servants, lived in this remote place. 'We all walked together to the mansion,' wrote Johnson, 'where we found one cottage for Sir Allan, and I think two more for the domestics and the offices. ... Our dinner, which was dressed in one of the other huts, was plentiful and delicate.' Boswell added: 'Sir Allan had made an apology at dinner that he had neither red wine nor biscuits, but that he expected both. Luckily the boat arrived with them this very afternoon. We had a couple of bottles of port and hard biscuits at night, after some roasted potatoes, which is Sir Allan's simple fare by way of supper.' The next day the travellers and Sir Allan, 'went with the boat to see oysters in the bed, out of which the boat-men forced up as many as were wanted.' Boswell noted: 'We found a great many of the small yellow whelks, and a good many small silver buckies [winkles].' That evening, one of Sir Allan's daughters played the harpsicord, while the other danced reels with Boswell and Young Coll. Early on the following morning Boswell went to the small but ancient chapel on the island, and prayed before the ruined altar. He then took a spade, and made a small grave for all the unburied human bones which were lying loose in the chapel, in the hope, as he told Johnson, that 'somebody would do as much for me'. After breakfast on 19th October, the travellers bade farewell to the Misses Maria and Sibella Maclean, and to Young Coll, who had been with them since they left Talisker in Skye. They then set out with Sir Allan in his 'good boat with four stout rowers' for Iona.

Partan Pie

Adapted from Mrs. Maciver's recipe for hot buttered crab.

For each person	
1 medium-cooked crab	nutmeg
1 tablespoon butter	salt and pinch of
2 tablespoons white breadcrumbs	cayenne pepper
2 tablespoons white wine or vinegar	juice of $\frac{1}{4}$ lemon
	sprigs of parsley

Prepare the crab by opening the apron and discarding the sack and gills, as these are inedible. Remove the claws, crack them, and pick out the meat. Remove the meat from the shell and body. Place all the meat in a bowl. Scrub the shell thoroughly, dry, and crack around the natural line with thumb and forefinger. Melt the butter in a small pan, add all the crab meat (brown and white), breadcrumbs, wine or vinegar, grated nutmeg, salt, cayenne, and lemon juice, and heat through. Pile into the shell, sprinkle with a few white crumbs and a little melted butter, and brown under a moderate grill. Serve hot. For smaller portions, serve in well-scrubbed scallop shells. Garnish with parsley.

Oyster Loaves

Adapted from Mrs. Cleland's recipe. This can be varied by using any other shellfish, of one sort or a mixture, with or without oysters.

4 small bread rolls	$\frac{1}{4}$ pint ($\frac{2}{3}$ cup) double cream
2 oz. ($\frac{1}{4}$ cup) butter	1 egg yolk
8 oysters, *or* 6 oz. of any other shellfish	salt and pepper
	lemon juice
4 tablespoons white wine	

Cut the top off the rolls, remove the crumbs with a spoon, brush the rolls with melted butter, and place in a warm oven for 10 minutes to crisp. Open the oysters, and poach for 2–3 minutes in their liquor. Remove, and keep warm. Add the white wine, and reduce. Mix together the cream and egg yolk, and stir into the wine. Allow to thicken without boiling. Season, and sharpen with lemon juice. Add the poached oysters (or other shellfish, if used). Reheat, and fill the rolls. Serve hot as a starter.

Iona Cathedral, by an unknown eighteenth-century artist
This was how Johnson and Boswell saw Iona or (to use the older name)
Icolmkill. The cathedral has now been restored, largely due to the efforts of the
Very Rev. Lord Macleod of Fuinary, M.C., D.D.

19th–20th October   Inchkenneth to Iona (or Icolmkill)

Host: John Macdonald, 'The Provost of Iona'

On their way from Inchkenneth to Iona the travellers' open boat made two stops on the Mull shore; at Gribun to see Mackinnon's Cave; and again near Bunessan to get some rum or whisky for the boatmen. During the second stop they had 'a repast of cold mutton, bread and cheese and apples, and punch'. They then rowed on to Iona, the holy isle of St. Columba, which was one of the main objectives of their tour. On landing, the travellers went with Sir Allan Maclean to the home of John Macdonald, known as 'The Provost of Iona', in whose barn they and their servants and boatmen spent the night. For supper, 'we had', wrote Boswell, 'cuddies and some oysters boiled in butter, that we might say we had fish and oyster sauce. Dr. Johnson eat none of that dish. We had roasted potatoes, of which I think he eat one; and he drank a mug of sweet milk.' The next morning, before eating their breakfast of 'milk, cheese, eggs, bread and butter,' the travellers made a full survey of the sacred remains of Iona,

and after breakfast viewed the Abbey or Cathedral. Johnson was so moved that he wrote his 'sublime passage', in which he stated: 'We are now treading that illustrious Island, which was once the luminary of the Caledonian regions, whence savage clans and roving barbarians derived the benefits of knowledge, and the blessings of religion. To abstract the mind from all local emotion would be impossible, if it were endeavoured; and would be foolish, if it were possible. ... Far from me and my friends, be such frigid philosophy as may conduct us indifferent and unmoved over any ground which has been dignified by wisdom, bravery, or virtue. That man is little to be envied, whose patriotism would not gain force upon the plain of *Marathon*, or whose piety would not grow warmer among the ruins of *Iona*!' The last sentence, embossed on a metal plaque, can now be seen on the road from the ferry to the Abbey on Iona, which the travellers left on 20th October after such a short but memorable visit.

Cloutie Dumpling

Adapted from Mrs. McLintock's recipe for 'Hunting Pudding', an ideal dish to serve to hardworking people, which made it a favourite meal for island boatmen. The 'clout' is the cloth in which the dumpling is boiled.

6 oz. ($1\frac{1}{2}$ cups) plain flour	2 oz. ($\frac{1}{2}$ cup) mixed peel
$\frac{1}{2}$ level teaspoon ground cinnamon	2 oz. (1 cup) white bread-crumbs
$\frac{1}{2}$ level teaspoon ground nutmeg	4 oz. ($\frac{3}{4}$ cup) prepared suet
1 level teaspoon bicarb. of soda	4 oz. ($\frac{1}{2}$ cup) caster (fine) sugar
$\frac{1}{2}$ level teaspoon salt	1 egg
3 oz. ($\frac{3}{4}$ cup) raisins	approx. $\frac{1}{4}$ pint ($\frac{2}{3}$ cup) buttermilk or sour milk
3 oz. ($\frac{3}{4}$ cup) currants	

Sieve the flour, spices, salt and soda into a bowl. Sir in the fruits, breadcrumbs, suet and sugar. Lightly beat the egg and add, with sufficient buttermilk or sour milk, to form a soft dropping mixture.

Have ready a large scalded pudding-cloth dusted with flour, which has been placed inside a bowl or colander to make a round shape. Place the mixture in the centre of the cloth, and draw up the edges, allowing plenty of room for the mixture to rise. Tie with string, and ease the folds to give a good round shape. Have ready a large pan with an enamel plate in the bottom. Put in the pudding and cover with boiling water. Boil gently for $2\frac{1}{2}$–3 hours, topping-up when necessary with more boiling water. Remove, leave to stand for a few minutes and peel off the cloth carefully. If desired, sprinkle the top with a mixture of sugar and cinnamon. Serves 6–8.

CAUDLE SAUCE   As an accompaniment to the pudding, Mrs. McLintock said: 'Let the sauce be White Wine and Sugar, or a Sack-caudle, as you please.' Mrs. Cleland gave the following recipe for Caudle Sauce: 'Take two Gills of white Wine, a little Nutmeg, sugar, and Lemon-peel, put it on the Fire, and when it is scalding hot, beat the yolks of two Eggs, and mix them with a little cold Wine; then mix all together; keep it stirring till it is scalding hot, then take it up, and pour it over the Pye or Tart.'

Dr. Johnson in his Travelling Dress, by Trotter
The scene is probably Mull and, although the artist may not have known it, the place looks very much like Rossal at Kinlochscridain, where the little Mull horses, or shelties (shown in the background), have been bred for at least 200 years.

20th–21st October   Iona to Rossal, Isle of Mull, staying *en route* at Ardchrishnish

Hosts: Rev. Neil Macleod, Minister of Kilfinichen, and his wife Margaret Maclean, at Ardchrishnish; and Dr. Alexander Maclean of Corrie-Kingairloch, and his wife Janet Fraser of Gualachoilish, at Rossal

From Iona the travellers, with Sir Allan Maclean, were rowed up Loch Scridain, and landed in Mull at Ardchrishnish, near the home of Rev. Neil Macleod, who 'had a black wig and a smart air, like an English parson'. His wife Margaret, the daughter of the former minister of the parish, Rev. Archibald Maclean, was 'a very well-behaved woman' who gave them 'an excellent supper'. The next morning, 21st October, the minister's neighbour, Donald Campbell of Ardtun, had breakfast with the travellers and, said Johnson, 'very obligingly furnished us with horses' to take them to Lochbuie by way of Rossal, the home of Dr. Alexander Maclean. This surgeon had succeeded his father as laird of Corrie in Kingairloch on the mainland, but did not take possession of his Morvern estate until 1775, when his lease or tack expired at Rossal. Appropriately, for a place deriving its name from *Hross-hóll*, the Norse for 'Horse-hill', the farm at Rossal was run by Dr. Maclean as a stud for breeding galloways and the little black Mull horses called shelties. This tradition of breeding shelties at Rossal is maintained by the present owner, Mr. Neil Macgillivray. Although Donald Campbell had supplied most of the horses for the travellers and their servants, Boswell wrote: 'I had a very pretty bay galloway belonging to Dr. Alexander Maclean. . . . He was one of the stoutest and most hearty men that I have seen, more of the farmer than of the doctor. He had a dinner prepared for us, so we could not refuse to stay and eat it. His wife did very well. We had a very good dinner.' Dr. Maclean was much impressed by Dr. Johnson, and said: 'This man is just a hogshead of sense'; and Boswell liked Dr. Maclean. 'He and I', wrote Boswell, 'took much to one another.' In common with his neighbour, namesake and contemporary, Dr. Alexander Maclean of Pennycross, with whom he was often confused, Dr. Alexander Maclean of Rossal had served as a surgeon in the Jacobite army at Culloden, but Boswell made no mention of this fact. From Rossal the travellers, with Sir Allan Maclean, set out for Lochbuie.

Jugged Hare

Also called 'muggled mawkin'. This is known to have been Dr. Alexander Maclean's favourite meal. Apart from the marinade, the ingredients are as follows:

1 young hare	$\frac{1}{2}$ pint ($1\frac{1}{4}$ cups) stock, made from the
2 oz. dripping	trimmings
1 oz. flour	2 tablespoons redcurrant jelly
salt and pepper	1 glass of port, optional

Joint the hare, saving the blood; or ask the butcher to do this. Mix together the ingredients for the marinade (see p. 45), add the jointed hare, turn occasionally and leave overnight to stand in a cool place. Melt the dripping in a heavy pan. Remove the joints from the marinade, dry, and place in hot fat to seal the outside. Remove to a casserole dish. Add flour to the dripping, and cook to a brown roux. Gradually add the stock, the marinade (with its vegetables) and stir to the boil. Add a little salt. Pour over the joints, cover the casserole, stand in a tin of water, and cook in a slow oven, Gas No. 2: 300°F., for 3–3$\frac{1}{2}$ hours. Remove, lift out the joints with a fork, strain the liquor into a saucepan, and reduce to about $\frac{3}{4}$ pint. Stir in the redcurrant jelly, and finally the blood. Reheat without boiling. Check the seasoning, and skim, if necessary. Stir in a glass of port, if used. Bawd Bree (or hare soup) can be made from trimmings.

Lochbuie House and Moy Castle, by G.E. (or E.G.)
On the right is Moy Castle, which looks the same today as it did in 1773. On the left is new Lochbuie House (built 1792), which is obscuring old Lochbuie House (built 1752), where Johnson and Boswell were entertained, and which is now used as a stable.

Retouched tracing of the stone over old Lochbuie House commemorating the 1773 visit

AFTER LEAVING MOY CASTLE, THE LOCHBUIE FAMILY RESIDED IN THIS HOUSE FROM 1752 TO 1790 AND IT WAS IN THIS HOUSE THAT DR JOHNSON AND MR BOSWELL WERE ENTERTAINED IN 1773 BY JOHN MACLAINE XVII LAIRD OF LOCHBUIE.

21st–22nd October   Rossal to Lochbuie, Isle of Mull

Hosts: John Maclaine of Lochbuie, 17th Baron of Moy, and his wife Isobel Maclean of Brolas, Lady Lochbuie

After a strenuous ride over the hills, Johnson and Boswell and Sir Allan Maclean arrived at the seat of John Maclaine of Lochbuie during the evening of 21st October. 'We had heard', wrote Boswell, 'a great deal of Lochbuie's being a great roaring braggadocio, a kind of Sir John Falstaff both in size and manners. . . . The truth is, that Lochbuie proved to be only a bluff, comely, noisy old gentleman, proud of his hereditary consequence, and a very hearty and hospitable landlord.' Although Lochbuie had not lived in nearby Moy Castle for thirty years, he had used its dungeon to imprison people, and his reputation for arrogance was built on this custom, and his habit of going to law on the slightest provocation. He was the last great feudal laird, and lived in a house he had built himself when he had deserted his castle in 1752. The supper he gave his guests was, according to Boswell, 'a poor one. I think a sort of stewed mutton was the principal dish. I was afterwards told that he has no spit, and but one pot, in which everything is stewed.' Lady Lochbuie, the sister of Sir Allan Maclean, did not impress Boswell, who said she wore 'a mean bed-gown, and behaved like the landlady of an alehouse'. The next morning she offered Johnson 'some cold sheep-head for breakfast', which caused her brother, Sir Allan, to be 'very angry at her vulgarity'. Johnson rejected her offer by replying 'No, Madam,' in 'a tone of surprise and anger'. Although the food was poor, Boswell acknowledged that Lochbuie was a delightful host and kept 'admirable port', of which he drank a full bottle, as well as a quantity of punch. Lochbuie was undoubtedly honoured by the visit of such celebrated guests, because he put a stone commemorating the event over the door of his house. After breakfast on 22nd October, the travellers said farewell to their hosts and Sir Allan on the shore of Mull, and took the ferry to Oban and the mainland. Their tour of the Hebrides had come to an end.

Hairst Bree

Also called Harvest Soup and Hotch-Potch. 'The excellence of this soup', wrote Mrs. Dods, 'depends mainly on the meat, whether beef or mutton, being perfectly fresh, and the vegetables being all young, and full of sweet juices.' Mrs. Cleland suggested the addition of 'Sellery or Endive, Broccoli or Asparagus when you can't get Pease'. It is a substantial dish, suitable for High Tea.

8 neck of lamb cutlets	6 oz. shelled peas
4 pints of water	½ cauliflower, sprigged
salt and pepper	½ small cabbage or lettuce,
6 small peeled turnips, diced	shredded
6 young carrots, diced	4 oz. shelled broad beans
12 syboes (spring onions)	chopped parsley

Place the cutlets and cold water in a large pan, bring slowly to the boil, remove scum, add about 2 teaspoons salt, cover, and simmer very gently for about 45 minutes. Add the diced turnips, carrots, onions, and half the peas, and simmer very gently for 1½ hours. Add the sprigged cauliflower, shredded cabbage or lettuce, the remainder of the peas, and the broad beans, and simmer until cooked, about 25 minutes. Check the seasoning, add plenty of freshly chopped parsley, and serve very hot. Serves 4–6.

Girls Washing, by McIan
Dr. Johnson, who was not particular about his clothes, or about changing them, made no mention of the way in which Highland women did their laundry in the streams.

22nd–24th October Lochbuie, Isle of Mull, to Inveraray, stopping *en route* at Oban (overnight) and Port Sonachan

Host: John Buchanan, landlord of the Argyll Arms Inn, Inveraray

The travellers had 'a fine passage' on the ferry from Mull to Oban, which was described by Faujas de St. Fond in 1786 as 'a little hamlet by the sea, consisting of six or seven scattered houses' whose inhabitants were renowned for catching large salmon. Johnson and Boswell stayed the night in the larger of Oban's two inns, 'a slated house of two storeys', which was (according to a modern inscription) on a site now occupied by Argyll House, on the corner of High Street and Argyll Square. The next morning, 23rd October, they rode to Loch Awe, which they crossed by ferry during a heavy shower. On landing at Port Sonachan they found a 'hut' or inn, where Boswell changed his sodden garments. 'Dr. Johnson resolutely kept on all his clothes, wet as they were, letting them steam before the smoky turf fire.' After a meal they rode on through the storm. 'The wind', wrote Johnson, 'was loud, the rain was heavy, and the whistling of the blast, the fall of the shower, the rush of the cataracts, and the roar of the torrent, made a nobler chorus of the rough music of nature than it had ever been my chance to hear before. . . . At last we came to Inveraray, where we found an inn, not only commodious, but magnificent.' This was the Argyll Arms, which still stands today. 'Even here', said Boswell, 'Dr. Johnson would not change his clothes. I put on a suit of our landlord's. . . . We supped well; and after supper, Dr. Johnson, whom I had not seen taste any fermented liquor during all our expedition, had a gill of whisky brought to him.' Johnson then made his famous remark about whisky: 'Come let me know what it is that makes a Scotsman happy.' They stayed for three nights at the Argyll Arms, where Johnson thought he had 'as good a room and bed as at an English inn'. Johnson spent part of his first morning there composing his 'Meditation on a Pudding'.

Salmon Trout

As neither Johnson nor Boswell named any food after they left Mull, the remaining recipes in this book have been selected from traditional Scottish sources. Mrs. Dods considered baked salmon trout 'a handsome dish'. Sea bass is excellent if it is cooked and served in the same way.

1 salmon trout, 3–4 lb.	1 onion, sliced
or cut of salmon, 2–2½ lb.	salt and pepper
2–3 oz. butter	parsley heads, and bay leaf

Remove the eyes, fins and the scales with a knife, and clean and gut. Trim the tail. Melt the butter gently. Brush the fish all over with the butter, and sprinkle with salt and pepper. Have ready a large piece of cooking foil brushed with butter. Lay the fish in the centre, and scatter the sliced onion, parsley heads and bay leaf on top. Close and seal the foil, twisting at the ends, making sure the head and tail are well buttered, or they will stick. Place in a tin, and cook in a very slow oven, Gas No. 1: 290°F., for 1¼–1½ hours, depending on the size and thickness of the fish. Carefully remove the foil, discard the sliced onion and parsley heads, and lift the fish onto a hot ashet. Serve with melted butter and wedges of lemon, or with Hollandaise Sauce. If to be served cold, remove the skin while the fish is warm, leave until cold and serve with Mayonnaise Sauce. Serves 6.

HOLLANDAISE SAUCE

6 crushed peppercorns	6 oz. just-melted butter
1 tablespoon wine vinegar	salt
2 egg yolks	lemon juice

Place the peppercorns in a small thick-bottomed pan, add vinegar and reduce. Add 1 tablespoon of cold water, and strain into the top of a double saucepan (or bowl standing over hot water). Add the egg yolks, and whisk until thick and creamy (*do not overheat*). Gradually whisk in the melted butter, add salt and lemon juice to taste and serve warm.

Inveraray Castle, by Griffith
The seat of the Campbells, Dukes of Argyll, as Johnson and Boswell saw it

24th–26th October In Inveraray, Argyllshire

Hosts: John Campbell, 5th Duke of Argyll, and his wife Elizabeth Gunning, Duchess of Argyll (formerly Duchess of Hamilton)

At breakfast on 25th October the travellers were joined by Rev. John Macaulay, minister of Inveraray, the brother of Rev. Kenneth Macaulay, with whom they had stayed at Cawdor. The minister went with them to Inveraray Castle, where they met the Duke of Argyll. 'What I admire here', said Johnson commenting on the castle, 'is the total defiance of expense'. Johnson was particularly impressed by the splendid display of Highland arms in the entrance hall, which form one of the great features of the castle to the present day. Dinner at the castle was rather embarrassing for Boswell, who some years earlier, during the great civil lawsuit known as the Douglas Cause, had attacked the very beautiful Duchess in a short work called *Dorando*. She had not forgiven this attack, and during dinner she not only ignored Boswell, but made her feelings completely clear by being 'very attentive to Dr. Johnson'. Boswell said: 'It was my duty to give about the soup, which I did with all imaginable ease, though conscious of the Duchess's peevish resentment.' He then tried to prove that he was immune to her snubs by proposing her health, although it was an unwritten rule at Inveraray Castle never to offer toasts to anybody. That evening, at the inn, the travellers were again joined by Rev. John Macaulay, whom Johnson rebuked for having the bad manners to interrupt him, but the minister came to breakfast the next morning and acted as though nothing had been said to offend him.

Veal Flory (or Florentine Pie)

Adapted from a recipe by Mrs. Maciver, who added currants and raisins to the dish.

for the rough puff pastry:
8 oz. (2 cups) plain flour
pinch of salt
6 oz. ($\frac{3}{4}$ cup) firm butter or margarine
6–7 tablespoons of cold water

for the filling:
1$\frac{1}{2}$ lb. lean veal
4 oz. streaky bacon
1 small onion, chopped
grated rind and juice of 1 lemon
4 oz. button mushrooms, washed
3 oz. ($\frac{3}{4}$ cup) stoned raisins
1 tablespoon chopped parsley
$\frac{1}{2}$ pint (1$\frac{1}{4}$ cups) stock, from trimmings
salt and pepper

ROUGH PUFF PASTRY Sieve the flour and salt into a bowl. Cut the fat into small lumps (the size of a walnut), add to the flour, and mix lightly without breaking up. Gradually add the water, and mix with a knife to form a fairly stiff dough. Turn onto a lightly-floured board, form into an oblong, and roll out to a long strip. Fold into 3, envelope style, half turn and roll out, and repeat twice more. Rest in a cool place for 30 minutes. If dough is sticky or the weather hot, rest it between rollings.

THE FILLING Trim and cut the veal into even-sized pieces (using trimmings to make $\frac{1}{2}$ pint of stock). Remove the rind from the bacon, and cut into 1-inch pieces. Mix together the veal, bacon, onion, rind and juice of lemon, mushrooms, raisins, parsley and salt and pepper. Place in a medium-sized pie-dish, and cover with cooled stock.

COMPLETION Roll out the pastry to about $\frac{1}{4}$ inch thick and 1$\frac{1}{2}$ inches wider all round than the pie-dish. Cut off a narrow strip of pastry; place round the damped rim of the pie-dish. Damp the strip, lift the remaining pastry on a rolling-pin, and ease on gently without stretching. Press down, trim, and flake the edge with a knife. Make a hole in the centre, and decorate with pastry leaves. Brush with beaten egg or milk. Bake in a pre-heated hot oven, Gas No. 7: 425°F., for 25 minutes. Reduce the temperature to Gas No. 4: 350°F., and cook for a further hour. Serves 4–6.

Loch Lomond, by Hill
Johnson and Boswell travelled down the western bank of this best known of all
Scottish lochs; they stayed at two places on its shores; and visited some of its islands.

26th–28th October — Inveraray to Cameron House, stopping *en route* at Tarbet and at Rossdhu, all on Loch Lomand

Hosts: Sir James Colquhoun of Luss, Bt., and his wife The Hon. Helen Sutherland, Lady Colquhoun, at Rossdhu; and Commissary James Smollett, and his wife Jean Clerk of Penicuik, at Cameron House

Mounted on one of the Duke of Argyll's stately horses Johnson left Inveraray with Boswell, also 'fully equipped', on 26th October, and rode over the mountains to Tarbet, where they had dinner. They then rode down the side of Loch Lomond to Rossdhu, the seat of Sir James Colquhoun, with whom they stayed the night. The next morning the travellers 'were furnished with a boat, and sailed about upon Loch Lomond, and landed on some of the islands', most of which were owned by Sir James. His wife, Lady Helen (who gave her name to the town of Helensburgh), was 'a very pious woman' and the conversation at dinner that day took 'a very religious turn', which allowed Johnson to deliver some ex-

cellent arguments. In the evening the travellers were taken a short distance down the loch in Sir James's coach to Cameron House, the home of Commissary James Smollett, a cousin of the celebrated novelist, Dr. Tobias Smollett, and here they stayed the night. 'Mr. Smollett', wrote Boswell, 'was a man of considerable learning, with an abundance of animal spirits; so that he was a very good companion for Dr. Johnson.' 'We have had', said Johnson, 'more solid talk here than at any place where we have been.' The next day, 28th October, a post-chaise was ordered, and they were on their way to Glasgow.

Scotch Trifle

This is included in a number of eighteenth-century cookery books. Mrs. Cleland made hers with a layer of apple purée, and Mrs. Frazer garnished the top of hers with a sprig of myrtle and preserved barberries.

1 medium sponge cake	*for the egg custard:*
3 heaped tablespoons of raspberry jam	$\frac{1}{2}$ pint ($1\frac{1}{4}$ cups) milk
	2 egg yolks
24 ratafia biscuits	1 tablespoon sugar
$\frac{1}{8}$ pint of sherry	vanilla pod or essence
juice and very finely grated rind of 1 lemon	$\frac{1}{2}$ pint ($1\frac{1}{4}$ cups) double cream
	1 tablespoon caster (fine) sugar
	whisky or Drambuie, to flavour
	cherries, angelica, or nuts

Cut the sponge cake through the centre, and spread with jam. Sandwich together, and place in a glass bowl. Crush half the ratafia biscuits, and place on top. Mix together the sherry, lemon juice and rind, and pour over the sponge and biscuits. Next make the custard. Heat the milk with the vanilla pod, or add a few drops of vanilla essence. Mix together the egg yolks and sugar.

Pour on the hot milk, stir, return to the saucepan, thicken without boiling. Remove the vanilla pod (if used), cool, and pour over the sponge. Leave until cold. Whisk the cream and caster sugar until thick, and flavour with whisky or Drambuie. Spread carefully over the custard, rounding in the centre. Arrange a border of ratafias around the bowl, and decorate with cherries, angelica, or pistachio nuts.

RATAFIA BISCUITS   Adapted from Mrs. Maciver's recipe for 'Ratafia Drops'.

2 egg whites	$\frac{1}{2}$ oz. rice flour
3 oz. ($\frac{1}{2}$ cup) ground almonds	few drops almond essence
4 oz. ($\frac{1}{2}$ cup) caster (fine) sugar	rice paper

Lightly whisk the egg whites, stir in the ground almonds, and sugar until smooth. Fold in the rice flour and essence. The consistency of the mixture should be stiff; if not, add a little more rice flour. Line a baking-tray with rice paper, and pipe the mixture into small circles or 'drops', about $\frac{3}{4}$ inch in diameter. Bake in the middle of a moderate oven, Gas No. 4: 350°F., for 15–20 minutes. Makes 24 small ratafias.

It is advisable to leave the ratafias to stand overnight before baking. They will form a skin on the outside, which prevents spreading when baking. Store in an airtight tin.

The Punch Bowl made in or about 1770 for the Saracen's Head Inn, Glasgow, and undoubtedly in use there when Johnson and Boswell were guests

Glasgow Cathedral from Duke Street, by Allan
Dr. Johnson, a staunch Episcopalian, admired St. Mungo's Cathedral, and was glad that it had been allowed to survive the Reformation without damage

28th–30th October Cameron House to Glasgow, stopping *en route* at Dumbarton

Host: The landlord of the Saracen's Head Inn, in the Gallowgate, Glasgow

On their way to Glasgow on 28th October the travellers stopped at Dumbarton to view the castle there, and though the approach to it was steep, 'Dr. Johnson ascended it with alacrity'. In Glasgow they stayed at the Saracen's Head Inn for two nights, and Johnson had the pleasure, after many days, of warming himself before a *coal* fire. The next morning they were joined for breakfast by three professors from Glasgow University, who took them on a tour of what Boswell called 'this beautiful city'. They called on Dr. William Leechman, the Principal of Glasgow University, who told Johnson that it was largely due to his influence the New Testament had been translated into Gaelic. Later that day, after entertaining four professors at their inn, the travellers had supper with John Anderson, Professor of Natural Philosophy, at the Professors' Court in the Old College. Johnson did not say that he thought Glasgow was beautiful, but he did write: 'The prosperity of its commerce appears by the greatness of many private houses, and a general appearance of wealth'; and he admired the Cathedral, Looking back on his tour of the Hebrides, he observed: 'A dinner in the Western Islands differs very little from a dinner in England, except that in place of tarts, there are always set different preparations of milk. This part of their diet will admit some improvement. Though they have milk and eggs and sugar, few of them know how to compound them into custard. Their gardens afford them no great variety, but they always have some vegetables on the table. ... Their suppers are, like their dinners, various and plentiful. The table is always covered with elegant linen. Their plates for common use are often of that kind of manufacture which is called cream-coloured, or queen's ware. They use silver on all occasions where it is common in England.'

Cream Cookies

In Scotland these are made from a rich yeast dough. They are split when cold, and filled with jam and cream, and sometimes dusted with icing-sugar.

1¼ lb. (5 cups) plain 'strong' flour
1 oz. fresh yeast
½ pint (1¼ cups) lukewarm milk
2 oz. (¼ cup) caster (fine) sugar
1 level teaspoon salt
4 oz. (½ cup) butter
2 eggs

Sieve the flour into a warm bowl. Blend the yeast with the lukewarm milk, and 1 teaspoon of the sugar. Pour onto the flour and mix to a dough. Cover, and leave to prove for 30 minutes in a warm place. Beat in the remaining sugar, the salt, butter and eggs until smooth. Cover, and return to a warm place for 30 minutes. Turn onto a floured board, and knead until smooth. Divide into 20 pieces and mould into rounds. Place well apart on a greased baking-tray. Cover, and leave in a warm place until double their size. Bake in a pre-heated hot oven, Gas No. 7: 425°F., for 15 minutes. Remove, and brush the tops with 1 tablespoon of sugar dissolved in 2 tablespoons of warm milk. Return to the oven for 3–4 minutes. Remove, and cool on a wire rack. Split, and fill with jam and cream, and, if liked, dust with icing-sugar.

30th October–8th November

Glasgow to Auchinleck House, stopping *en route* at Loudoun Castle and Treesbank

Hosts: John Campbell, 4th Earl of Loudoun, and his mother Margaret Dalrymple, Countess of Loudoun; and James Campbell of Treesbank, and his wife Mary Montgomerie; and Alexander Boswell, Lord Auchinleck, and his second wife (and cousin) Elizabeth Boswell, Lady Auchinleck

Johnson and Boswell left Glasgow on 30th October, and set out for Ayrshire. As they approached Galston, Boswell sent his servant Joseph ahead with a message for the Earl of Loudoun asking if they could dine with him. The Earl, according to Boswell, 'jumped for joy' at the prospect of entertaining unexpected guests, and he and his 94 year old mother received the travellers well. After this visit to Loudoun Castle, they moved on a few miles to the home of Boswell's brother-in-law, James Campbell of Treesbank, where they stayed for two nights. On 2nd November, the travellers left Treesbank, and went by post-chaise to Auchinleck House, the home of Boswell's father, Lord Auchinleck, a judge, who was slightly older than Johnson. Here they stayed until 8th November. Boswell was anxious that his father and Johnson would get on well together. All was quiet for two or three days, and then Lord

Auchinleck made a controversial remark, which brought a sharp rebuke from Johnson. This was followed the next day by a more spirited contest in the library. As both men had such strong but opposing views on religion and politics, a contest, or 'collision' as Boswell called it, was almost inevitable. Lord Auchinleck later referred to Johnson as 'Ursa Major'—'The Big Bear'. Dr. Johnson gave quicker point to his resentment by refusing to accompany Boswell and Lord Auchinleck to the Presbyterian Church on Sunday, 7th November. Nonetheless, Johnson admitted in his *Journal* that Lord Auchinleck had 'advanced the value of his lands with great tenderness to his tenants', and when Johnson left for Edinburgh with Boswell on 8th November, Lord Auchinleck bade farewell with 'the dignified courtesy of an old baron'.

Burnt Cream

Adapted from Mrs. Cleland's recipe.

1 pint (2½ cups) single cream	5 egg yolks
1 vanilla pod, or cinnamon stick	1 rounded tablespoon sugar
strip of orange rind	4 oz. (½ cup) caster (fine) sugar

Place the cream in the top of a double saucepan with the vanilla pod (or cinnamon stick) and the orange rind, and heat slowly. Beat together the egg yolks and 1 tablespoon sugar. Pour the hot cream onto the egg yolk mixture, and stir well. Strain back into the top of the saucepan, and cook gently, stirring all the time until thick. Pour into a shallow dish, and leave overnight until cold. Sprinkle the top liberally with caster sugar. Place under a very hot grill and caramelize the top. Remove, and serve quite cold.

Scotch Flummery

Also adapted from a recipe by Mrs. Cleland.

2 oz. (½ cup) washed currants	2 tablespoons caster (fine) sugar
2 tablespoons dry sherry	1 teaspoon rosewater, *or* orange flower water
1 pint single cream	little grated nutmeg
5 egg yolks	

Macerate the currants in the sherry. Heat the cream to blood-heat. Mix together the egg yolks, sugar, rosewater (or orange flower water) and nutmeg in a bowl. Pour on the heated cream, stir, and strain into a lightly greased mould. Cover with paper or foil. Steam *very gently* for 30–40 minutes, until set. Remove, leave to stand for a few minutes, turn out carefully onto a warm plate, and sprinkle with currants. Serve hot. Serves 4–6.

The Contest at Auchinleck, by Rowlandson
Lord Auchinleck lifts his hand to protect himself from a book aimed by Dr. Johnson, while James Boswell prays for help. This is a greatly exaggerated version of the dispute between Johnson and his host.

9th–22nd November   Auchinleck to Edinburgh: and finally to Blackshiels, stopping *en route* at Cranston

Dr. Johnson's hosts: James Boswell, and his wife Margaret Montgomerie, in Edinburgh; and Sir John Dalrymple, Bt., and his wife Elizabeth Hamilton, Lady Dalrymple, at Cranston

On the evening of 9th November, the travellers returned to their starting point at James's Court in Edinburgh 'after an absence of eighty-three days'. Johnson stayed there as the Boswells' guest for twelve days, during which time he met many eminent Scots he had not seen before, and a few that he had, including Lord Monboddo. Indeed, so many celebrated people called to compliment the travellers on their return that Johnson told Boswell: 'I am really ashamed of the congratulations which we receive. We are addressed as if we had made a voyage to Nova Zembla, and suffered five persecutions in Japan.' None the less, he was glad to see once more some of the Edinburgh *literati*, and had long discussions with Dr. William Robertson, Lord Elibank and Rev. Dr. Hugh Blair. He also dined with Sir Alexander Dick at Prestonfield House, now one of Edinburgh's most attractive private hotels. On 20th November, Johnson left Edinburgh, and went twelve miles with Boswell to Cranston to stay with Sir John and Lady Dalrymple. Johnson in talking to Boswell was extremely rude about Lady Dalrymple, whom he called 'an odious woman' because she had inadvertently confused him about cuts of meat. The next day they visited Borthwick Castle (now beautifully restored), and they spent that night at the inn at Blackshiels, which was only two miles from Cranston, because Johnson did not want to see the Dalrymples again. The following day, 22nd November, Boswell helped Johnson aboard the stagecoach going to England, and the famous visit to Scotland was over. Later, when writing to Boswell, Dr. Johnson said: 'I will not send compliments to my friends by name. . . . Tell them, as you see them, how well I speak of Scotch po teness and Scotch hospitality and Scotch beauty, and of everything Scotch, but Scotch oatcakes, and Scotch prejudices.'

Gaelic Coffee Cake

A modern recipe, created by the author of this book.

for the cake mixture
4 oz. (½ cup) butter or margarine
4 oz. (½ cup) caster (fine) sugar
2 eggs
1–2 tablespoons of coffee essence, *or* strong black coffee
4 oz. (1 cup) self-raising flour (sieved)

for the coffee syrup and decoration
¼ pint (⅔ cup) water
4 oz. (½ cup) sugar
½ gill (⅓ cup) strong black coffee
2 tablespoons whisky
½ pint (1¼ cups) double cream
1 tablespoon caster (fine) sugar
whisky or Drambuie, to flavour
walnuts and cherries

THE CAKE   Place the butter or margarine in a mixing-bowl, and beat until soft. Add the sugar, and continue beating until the mixture is light and creamy. Gradually beat in the eggs, adding a little of the flour with the second egg. Beat in the coffee. Using a metal spoon, fold in the flour. Place in a well-greased 8-inch ring-mould. Bake in a pre-heated moderate oven, Gas No. 4: 350°F., for 30–35 minutes.

THE COFFEE SYRUP   Place the water and sugar in a saucepan over a low heat, and stir until dissolved. Bring to the boil, and cook for 3–4 minutes. Remove from the heat, and stir in the coffee and 2 tablespoons of whisky.

TO COMPLETE   Carefully remove the cake from the ring-mould, pour the flavoured syrup into the mould, gently return the cake into the mould, and leave to soak up the syrup, preferably overnight. Turn out onto a serving-plate. Place the cream and sugar in a bowl, and whisk until thick. Stir in the whisky or Drambuie, to flavour. Spread the cream carefully all over the moist cake, and decorate with walnuts and cherries. Serves 6–8.

The Journalist, by Rowlandson
In a moment of self-importance at Auchinleck, Boswell thinks of his proposed *Life of Johnson*. In his pocket is Ogden's *Sermons on Prayer*, which appears in many of Rowlandson's cartoons.

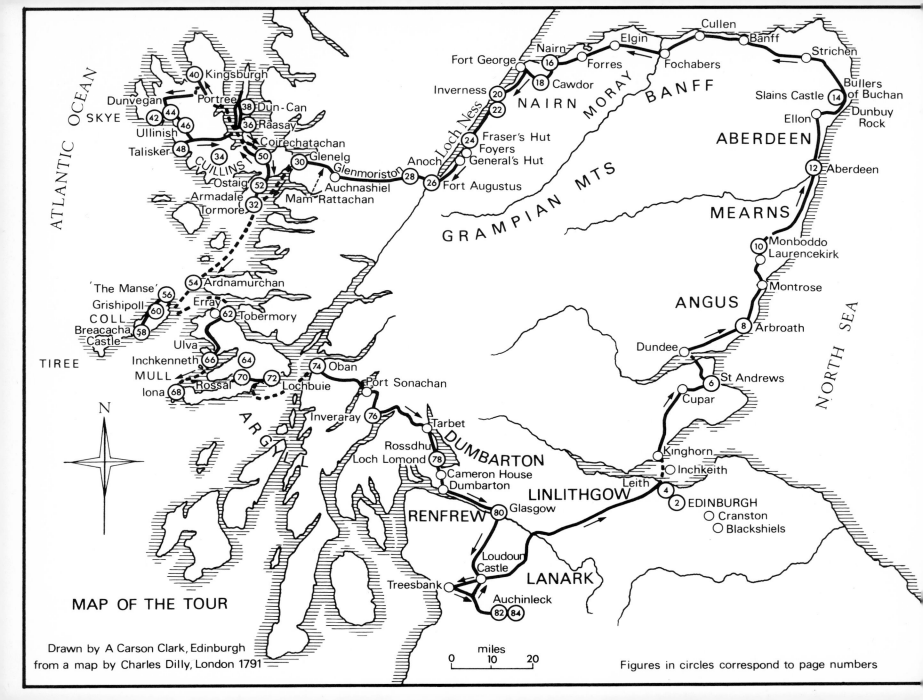

MAP OF THE TOUR

Drawn by A Carson Clark, Edinburgh
from a map by Charles Dilly, London 1791

Figures in circles correspond to page numbers